THE GOD
OF
JESUS CHRIST

THE GOD
OF
JESUS CHRIST

Meditations on God in the Trinity

Joseph Cardinal Ratzinger
Archbishop of Munich

TRANSLATED BY
ROBERT J. CUNNINGHAM

FRANCISCAN HERALD PRESS
1434 WEST 51st STREET • CHICAGO, 60609

The God of Jesus Christ, Meditations on God in the Trinity by
Joseph Cardinal Ratzinger translated by Robert J. Cunningham,
originally published in German *Der Gott Jesus Christi, Betrachtungen uber den Dreieinigen Gott,* Kosel-Verlag, 1976. Copy-
right © 1979 by Franciscan Herald Press, 1434 West 51st Street,
Chicago, Illinois 60609.

Library of Congress Cataloging in Publication Data
Ratzinger, Joseph.
  The God of Jesus Christ.

  Translation of Le Dieu de Jesus-Christ.
  1. Trinity—Sermons. 2. Catholic Church—Sermons.
3. Sermons, English—Translations from French. 4. Sermons, French—Translations into English. I. Title.
BT113.R3713   231   78-16275
ISBN 0-8199-0697-2

MADE IN THE UNITED STATES OF AMERICA

*To My
Classmates
On the Twenty-Fifth
Anniversary of
Our Ordination to
the Priesthood
1951-1976*

Contents

Preface

In the spring of 1973, I gave a series of Lenten sermons in St. Emeram's Church at Regensburg. This gave me an opportunity to test in a practical way some principles I had recently developed in a book entitled Dogma and Preaching (Dogma und Verkündigung), *which was published that same year at Munich. Chapters 1 and 3 of the present work are a revised and edited version of the 1973 sermons. The sermons, in turn, were based on ideas I had sketched out in the "Announcement of God in Today's World," a section of* Dogma and Preaching.

Chapter 2 is the result of some thoughts about Advent that I delivered at a gathering in Freiburg im Breisgau in December 1972. In preparing Chapter 2 I also made use of a sermon given at Regensburg in 1975 as part of the commemoration of the Council of Nicaea. It is also based on a lecture I gave at Easter over the Bavarian radio.

I also made use of all the materials in the present book (but in a different order) during retreats preached at Bad Imnau, at the seminary of Cologne, and at Maria Laach. During the retreats the materials achieved the unified form in which they now appear in this book. Despite the many insufficiencies that are a consequence of the origin of these meditations, I hope that they may help build a bridge between theology and spirituality, and that they may help others assimilate in a personal way the faith the Church proclaims.

Pentling, the feast of Saints Peter and Paul, 1976.

+ Joseph RATZINGER

CHAPTER 1
God

GOD HAS NAMES

We all recall when Yuri Gargarin returned from his journey into space — the first in the history of humanity — and remarked that nowhere had he seen God. Now at that time (1961), even thoughtful atheists realized that this was not a very valid argument for denying the existence of God. We had no need for Gargarin to know that we can neither feel God with our hands nor see him through a telescope, and that he does not live on the moon or Saturn or some other planet or star. This is quite apart from the fact that such a journey into space, even if a grandiose performance for humanity, scarcely went a few steps beyond our doorway with respect to the immensity of the universe. After all, Gargarin's journey offered to our eyes much less than we already knew about the universe as a result of mathematical calculations and observation.

In a much deeper way the agonizing feeling of God's absence that is characteristic of all of us today was expressed centuries ago in a Jewish fable. According to the story, one day the prophet Jeremiah, with the help of his son, succeeded in creating a living man by combining some words and letters. On the forehead of the Golem — the man created by man — were inscribed the letters used to unveil the mystery of creation: "Yaweh is Truth." The Golem removed one of the seven letters of the Hebrew phrase, and the inscription then read: "God is dead." The prophet and his son were filled with terror and asked the Golem what he was up to. And the new man replied: "Since you have learned to create man, God is dead. My life means the death of God. For where man is all-powerful, God no longer has any power."[1]

This old Jewish story, which was conceived during the Christian Middle Ages, reveals the torments of humanity in a technological age. Human beings have all power over the earth. They expose the functions of the earth to the light of day, and they know the laws that govern its path in space. Their knowledge is their power: They have so to speak the power to take the world apart and put it back together by themselves. For humans the world is a combination of functions that they utilize and force to serve them. In a world thus exposed to the light of day, there is no longer room for God's intervention. Every assistance given to humanity can only come from other human beings. Since power over the world is only found in human beings, there is no longer a God.

Such thoughts clearly reveal at the same time a fundamental aspect of the problem human beings have in knowing God. Knowledge of God in the end is not a matter of pure theory but is in the first place a matter of practice and of life. It depends on the relationship that human beings establish between themselves and the world, between themselves and their own lives. The problem of power thus represents only a single aspect, which has been preceded by more profound decisions about the relationship to the *I,* to the *You,* and the *We,* as humans experience whether or not they are loved or rejected. These basic experiences and decisions in the reciprocal overlappings of the I, the You, and the We determine whether or not human beings see or do not see, in the fact that the other Person is already there and preexists, a rivalry, a danger, or a reason for confidence. These experiences also determine whether in the long run, human beings will find themselves forced to contend with that witness or whether they will be capable of saying yes to him out of respect and in thanksgiving.

This idea leads to the real point of departure of our problem about the existence of God, who himself is placed far upstream in the river of controversy about the proofs of his existence. For this reason I should like to clear the matter up a little more by starting out from the viewpoint of the history of religion. In the religious history of humanity, which is totally identified with human cultural history even in higher civilizations, God appears everywhere as a Being who is all eyes, like vision itself.[2] The image of the eye of God, which Christian art has rendered familiar to us, has kept alive this archaic concept: God is an Eye, God is Sight. Under this image we also rediscover a primitive feeling of human beings: They know they are recognized. They know that they are never totally under cover; that their lives are open and delineated in a Sight; and that this is the case everywhere, for there is no possibility of shielding themselves or of escaping scrutiny. Humans know that to live means to be seen. One of the most beautiful psalms of the Old Testament expresses in a prayerful form this conviction, which has accompanied humans throughout history:

> Lord, you have probed me and you know me;
> you know when I sit and when I stand;
> you understand my thoughts from afar.
> My journeys and my rest you scrutinize,
> with all my ways you are familiar.
> Even before a word is on my tongue,
> behold, O Lord, you know the whole of it.
> Behind me and before, you hem me in
> and rest your hand upon me . . . .
> Where can I go from your spirit?
> From your presence where can I flee?
> If I go up to the heavens, you are there;
> if I sink to the nether world, you are present there.
> If I take the wings of the dawn,
> if I settle at the farthest limits of the sea,
> even there your hand shall guide me,
> and your right hand hold me fast.
> If I say, "Surely the darkness shall hide me,
> and night shall be my light — "
> for you darkness itself is not dark,
> and night shines as the day . . . . (Psalm 139: 1–5; 7–12)

As I stated above, human beings may resent very sharply the fact that they are seen thus from all sides. They may believe themselves totally exposed and feel annoyed about it. They may sense a danger in it and feel limited in their existence. Such a feeling then may reach the point of exasperation, and become intense to the point of a passionate struggle against that witness, who is resented like someone envying us our freedom as well as the unlimited nature of our will and our actions. But the very opposite also can happen: Human beings, who are made to love, may find in the presence surrounding them on all sides the refuge toward which their entire being aspires. They may see in it a means of overcoming the solitude that, when all is said and done, no one is ever capable of suppressing. For solitude is truly something in contradiction with our very being, which cries out for another person and for a shared presence. In this secret presence humanity may find a reason for the confidence that makes us live.

Here is where human beings decide on the response to make to the question of God's existence. It depends on the way in which human beings conceive of their lives from the very beginning. On the one hand, do they wish not to be seen? Do they wish to remain totally alone in the hope that they "will be like God"? Or on the other hand, despite their insufficiencies and in fact precisely because of them, do they feel grateful toward the one who supports them and bears all their solitude? Whether the first or second of these responses is given depends on different causes. The response depends on the experiences that have characterized the I in its relationship with the You. For such a relationship can appear either like love or like a threat. Everything depends on the aspect under which God first appears to us — as the watcher who inspires terror and implacably contrives punishment for us, or as the creative love that awaits us. Everything depends also on the decisions by which we as human beings in the course of our lives accept the responsibility of transforming our experiences of the past.

From the preceding reflection we should probably retain the following point: the question of knowing whether God exists, and the question of knowing *who* and *what* he is cannot be kept apart from each other. We cannot begin to prove or challenge the existence of God, and then later start to wonder who and what he is. The content of our image of God determines in a decisive way whether our knowledge of him can expand or not. But inasmuch as that knowledge and that content limit or open up our area of knowledge about ourselves as human beings, they become so deeply involved in the way we take basic positions about human life that in this respect theory alone is powerless.

In view of all this, let's now ask ourselves a question: what does the God of the Bible look like? Who is he precisely? In the history of the biblical revelation in the Old and New Testaments, God's appearance to Moses, as narrated in Chapter 3 of the Book of Exodus, has been shown to be continuously and progressively fundamental.

In this passage we should pay attention first of all to the historical and local background. The historical background appears in the divine statement: "I have witnessed the affliction of my people in Egypt and have heard their cry of complaint against their slave drivers, so I know well what they are suffering" (Ex. 3:7). God is the defender of the law. He justified the powerless against the powerful. This is his true countenance. This is the heart of Old Testament legislation, which constantly places the widow, the orphan, and the stranger under God's protection. We also find this concept at the heart of the preaching of Jesus as he defended the situation of the accused, the condemned, and the sick, who were thus placed under God's protection.

Even Jesus' struggle to preserve his own meaning of the Sabbath follows this same concept. (This is the last example I shall give on this point.) In the Old Testament the Sabbath is the day of freedom for all creatures, the day when human beings and animals, slaves and masters, all

GOD

take their rest. It is the day on which, in the very heart of a world filled with inequality and the lack of freedom, the brotherly communion of all creatures is restored. It is the day when Creation, only for the interval of a sigh, returns to its point of departure; it is the day when the whole world is free in the freedom of God. Jesus' action with respect to the Sabbath was not against the Sabbath, but rather a struggle to restore its original meaning. The Sabbath was to remain a day of divine freedom; it should not become in the hands of the casuists a day of petty torments, that is, the opposite of what it was intended to be.[3]

The setting of Chapter 3 of the Book of Exodus was the desert. For Moses as for Elias and Jesus, this was the place of the summons and shaping. Without a withdrawal from everyday agitation, without a confrontation with the power of solitude, there was no experience with God. If the first viewpoint — the historical background — has led us to acknowledge that the greedy, egotistical heart cannot recognize God, the second authorizes us to state that the loud, inattentive, and impatient heart cannot find him either.

Let us come now to the heart of the matter. God gave a name to himself in front of Moses and clarified it in the formula: "I am who am."[4] This event is inexhaustible. The entire history of our faith, including Jesus' confession of God, has been only a renewal of the interpretation of these words, which at the same time have taken on an ever-increasing profundity. In any case one thing right away was clear: by this explanation the name Yahweh was clearly and precisely distinguished from the divine names that existed at that time in that area. That name was not a name like many others because the one who bore it was not a being among many similar beings. His name was a mystery

— 13 —

that placed him beyond all possible comparison. "I am who am" — that meant nearness and power over the present and the future. God was not a prisoner of what had taken place "from all eternity." He had always been present: "I am." He is both of all times and ahead of all times. I can invoke that God here and now; he is the God of now who responds to my now.

Centuries later, at the end of the period of the long exile of the Jews, another aspect of God was decisive. The powers of the world which openly boasted that Yahweh was dead were dethroned overnight. They passed away, but he remained. He "is." His "I am" was not only the real presence of God, but it was at the same time a mark of his persistence. He was and is at every crossing — yesterday, today, and tomorrow. Eternity is not the past but it is precisely an absolute certitude in which we can trust, a constancy that always sustains us. God "is" — and this is what concerns us once again in a period when we completely confuse the present and the good, the modern and the true. Time is not God. God is the Eternal One, and time is an idol as soon as it becomes an object of adoration.[5]

It becomes necessary now to ask another question, one that is more basic and more general: in fact, what does the expression *name of God* mean? Could the fact that the God of the Old Testament had names be more than a reminiscence of a polytheistic world in which Israel's faith gradually had to overcome obstacles to attain its own shape? Each of the names of God — and they were very numerous in the ancient layers of the Jewish tradition — disappeared during the evolutionary course of the Old Testament faith. This fact seems to speak in favor of such a concept. Of course, Yahweh's name was maintained, but in view of the Second Commandment it had no longer been spoken since long before the time of Jesus. The New Testament no longer knew any precise name for God because in the Greek Old Testament, Yahweh's name had been replaced from the beginning to the end by the expression *the Lord.*

This situation, however, only describes one aspect of things. It is true that the different names of God disappeared as soon as people emerged from the polytheistic world of early times. On the other hand, the concept that God had a name played a decisive role in the New Testament. In Chapter 17 of the Gospel of St. John, which we are justified in calling in many respects the high point in in the development of New Testament faith, "the name of God" is repeated four times. The main section of the statement is framed in verses 6 and 26, by the very words of Jesus proclaiming that his mission is to announce to humanity the name of God. Jesus appears like the new Moses who is the first to do wholly and truly what in the event of the burning bush was only begun in a partial and hidden way.

What then does the name of God mean? Perhaps if we begin with its opposite we shall be better able to understand what it is all about. The Book of the Apocalypse speaks of the enemy of God, the beast. The beast — the counterpower — does not bear a name but a number — 666 — the seer tells us. The beast is a number and translates into numbers. What that means is known to us who have experienced the world of the concentration camps: Its horror was due to the fact that the camps obliterated faces, annihilated history, and turned human beings into interchangeable parts of a huge machine. Human beings were identified by their functions, nothing more. Today we must fear that the concentration camps were only a prelude, and that the world, in accord with the universal law of the machine, may adapt itself completely to the organization of the concentration camps. For in a place where only functions exist, human beings can only be a kind of a function. The machines that human beings have constructed will stamp on people the sign of the machines. It is necessary to render human beings legible to the computer, and this is only possible if human beings are translated into figures. Everything else remaining in human beings becomes unimportant. Whatever is not a function is nothing. The beast is a number that transforms people into numbers. But God has names and calls us by name. He is a Person who seeks other persons. He has a countenance and he seeks our countenances. He has a heart, and he seeks our hearts. For him we are not functions of the great machine of the world; precisely those persons who have no automatic function are his people. To have a name means the possibility of being called, and it means communion. For this reason Christ is the true Moses, the fulfillment of the revelation of the name. He did not come to bring a new word as a name, but much more; he was himself the face of God, he was the name of God; he was the possibility even for God to be called "you," to be called as a Person and as a heart. His own name *Jesus* brought to its conclusion the mysterious name of the burning bush. Now it appeared clearly that God had not left off speaking, that he had only temporarily broken off speech. For the name Jesus in its Hebrew form contains the word *Yahweh* and adds to it "God saves." "I am who am" has meant since the time of Jesus: "I am the one who saves you." His being is Salvation.

According to the calendar of the Church, March 3 is the feast of St. John of God whose work — the Brothers Hospitallers — has the care of the sick as its mission.* From the moment of John's conversion, his life consisted only of the gift of himself to others: to those who suffered and were rejected as well as to the poorest of his generation, including those suffering from mental illness as well as prostitutes to whom he sought to offer the possiblity of a new life. Reading his letters gives us an overwhelming impression of the passion with which the man wore himself out for the oppressed:

> I work in debt and am a prisoner for Christ's love. My financial debts weigh so heavily upon me that I often do not dare leave the house because of the demands for payment in which I am engulfed. And when I see so many poor men, my brothers, who suffer beyond their strength and are overwhelmed by a distress of body and soul while I am unable to help them, a dreadful affliction takes possession of me. But I build on Christ, for he knows my heart.[6]

It seems to me quite significant that to this man has been given the surname "of God." In fact, through a life that was consumed for the sake of human beings there appears in an incomparably luminous way what God is, that is, the God of the burning bush and the God of Jesus Christ. He is justice for those to whom no justice has been given.

---

*St. John of God was a Spanish soldier who suddenly left the world to devote himself to the care of the poor and the sick. He died in 1550.

THE GOD OF JESUS CHRIST

He is the Eternal One and the Person who is close to us. He has names and the power to give names to others. May we succeed in being forever men and women "of God" so that we can know God better and become for others a path that leads to the knowledge of God.

GOD IS ONE IN THREE PERSONS

How often have we made the sign of the cross, invoking without realizing it the name of the trinitarian God? In its original meaning that sign means — every time we make it — the renewal of our baptism and the renewal of the words by which we became Christians. It assimilates into our personal life what was given to us in baptism without our intervention or reflection. In baptism water was poured over us, and at the same time these words were spoken: "I baptize you in the name of the Father, and of the Son, and of the Holy Spirit." The Church makes people Christians by calling on the name of the trinitarian God. Thus since its beginning the Church has expressed what is truly decisive in the essence of a Christian, namely, the faith in one God in three persons.

This disappoints us. It is so remote from our lives! It is so useless, so unintelligible! Granted that we expect to receive from brief formulas something attractive and exciting, something whose importance for human beings and their lives is immediately indispensible. All the same what *a* is really at stake in this instance is not what is said about the Church or about human beings but rather what is said about God. The whole orientation of this sign does not have to do with our hopes, fears, or desires but rather with God and his majesty and power. The first article of Christian faith and the basic orientation of Christian conversion is that God exists.

But what does that mean? What does it mean in our everyday life, in the world that is ours? Well, it means one thing first of all: God exists, and thus the "gods" are not God. We must adore him and no one else. But have not all the gods died off in any case — and long ago? Isn't that obvious anyway and hence of no significance?

Whoever looks reality in the face has no reply by asking a contrary question. In our own time does no one serve idols any more? Is only God adored, and is nothing adored in opposition to him? After the "death of God," are gods not revealing themselves with a power that is quite disturbing? That simultaneousness of events was expressed in an impressive way by Martin Luther in his Great Catechism:

What does it mean to have a God, and what is God?
Reply: To have a God means to have something in sight of which we ought to arm ourselves with everything that is

good and in which we should find refuge in time of trouble. Thus to have a God means simply to trust him with all our heart and to believe, as I've often said, that only trust and faith from the heart make God as well as an idol.[7]

In what shall we place our trust, and in what shall we then believe? Money, power, fame, public opinion, sex — have not all these things become powers before which human beings bend their knees, powers which human beings serve as if they were gods? Would not the world be a different place if such gods were cast down from their thrones?

God is. This means that above all our ambitions and all our interests there is the sovereignty of truth and of the law. There is the adoration of God himself; it is the true adoration that protects us from the dictatorship of ambition, and it alone can protect us from the dictatorship of idols.

God is. This means also that all of us are his creatures. To be sure, we are only creatures, but precisely as creatures we truly derive our origin from God. We are creatures that he has willed into being and promised to eternity. Even our neighbor — perhaps that unattractive individual right next to me — is one of his creatures.

Human beings do not appear just as a result of chance nor as a result of a mere struggle for existence that leads to the victory of human ambitions and of persons able to assert themselves. Instead, human beings appear as a result of the creative love of God. God is. And here we must underline the little word *is* to signify that God truly exists. He exists, is active, acts, and he is capable of taking action. He is not a distant source nor a vague "direction of our transcendentality." He has not resigned before the challenge of the big machine of this world. He has not lost his whole function because everything functions by itself. The world is, and remains, his world; the present is his time, not the past. He is capable of acting, and he really takes action — now, in our world and in our lives. Do we trust him? Do we look on him as a reality in the computation of our lives and our everyday experience? Have we grasped the meaning of the first tablet of the Ten Commandments, which is truly the basic requirement of human life according to the first three requests of our Father? These requests sum up the first tablet of the law in order to make of it the main orientation of our spirit and our lives.

God is. Christian faith adds that God is as the Father, Son, and Holy Spirit. For most Christians an embarrassed silence surrounds this center of their faith. Hasn't the Church gone too far in this matter? Wouldn't it be better to leave to something so great and impenetrable its characteristic of inaccessibility? Besides, can such a reality mean anything to us? Of course, this article of faith is and remains the way to express the fact that God is the Other, that he is infinitely greater than we, and that he goes beyond our thinking and our whole being. But if he had nothing to tell us, his context would not have been revealed to us. And in the same way, he could only be formulated in human speech because he has sufficiently penetrated into the thought and lives of human beings.

What does all this mean? Let's begin where God himself began. He calls himself Father. Human fatherhood can give us an idea of what he is. But in places where there is any fatherhood, and where true fatherhood is no longer felt — either as a biological phenomenon or as a human and spiritual phenomenon — to talk of God the Father in such places is to talk in a void. Wherever human fatherhood has disappeared, God can no longer be expressed or thought of. God has not died, but in human beings something has totally died that is a necessary condition for God's existence in the world. The crisis of fatherhood which we are living through today constitutes the heart of the human crisis that is threatening us. Where fatherhood no longer appears as anything other than a biological accident without human recourse, or where it appears as a tyranny to be rejected, we find a wound deep in the very fiber of human existence. To be fully human we need a father in the true sense of the word, the way the father has appeared throught faith. Being a father means to have a responsibility toward another person. It does not mean that the father should dominate the other person but should convey to him or to her true freedom. A father's love should not seek to take possession of another, and yet should not confirm the other person's remaining just as he or she was "on arrival," pretending that this is being done for the sake of liberty. This love wants the other to find his or her most personal truth, which is in his or her creator. This manner of being a father is possible, of course, only on condition that we accept the idea of ourselves as children. To consent to Jesus' statement that ". . . one is your Father, who is in heaven" (Matt. 23:9) is an internal condition needed for men to be capable of being fathers in a good sense — not in dominion over others but in a spirit of responsibility toward the truth, a responsibility freely devoted to God and which can thus give unselfishly to another his liberty for God in whom we find our own being.

Of course, we must complete our thought. The fact that in the Bible God appears basically under the image of a "Father," includes the fact that the mystery of the maternal also has its source in God. The mystery of maternity reverts as much to God, or when it is distorted, departs as much as does paternity. We can understand that a human being the "image of God" here in its real, very practical context. A human being is not the image of God as an abstraction. That would only bring us to an abstract God. A human being is the image of God in his or her concrete reality which is as a relationship: He or she is so as a father, as a mother, or as a child, that is as a son or daughter. In such a perspective these names, when applied to God, are "images," but they are so because a human being is an "image," and they are so out of the requirement of the reality within them. They are images that require an "Image," and in this respect they may just as well realize God as signify his "death." The human incarnation of humanity cannot be disassociated from humanity's knowledge of God, precisely because a human being is the "image" of God. At the point where the human element in a person is destroyed, the image of God suffers. The dissolution of the concept of fatherhood and motherhood, which people would like to relegate to the dungeons of the past or at least diminish to a mere biological moment that does not concern a human being as a human being — this tendency is tied to the dissolution of childhood, which is supposed to give way from the very beginning to total equality. It is a program of hybridation that seeks in one swoop to remove humanity from its biological place and subject it totally to slavery. This program affects the very roots of the human being and the roots of our capacity to think of

God. Wherever God is not represented, he can no longer be thought of. Wherever human thought uses all its strength to make the representation of God impossible, a "proof for the existence of God" can no longer have anything to say to us.

Of course, when we make such critical reflections about the present day, we should not exaggerate. On the one hand, we should not forget that exemplary fathers and mothers still exist today. Moreover, certain great figures like Janusz Korczak and Mother Teresa show how in our own period of history it is possible to assume the true nature of a father or a mother without being one in a biological sense. On the other hand, we should always keep in mind the fact that a totally pure realization of this concept has always been an exception, and that the image of God in humanity has always been defiled and distorted. And for this reason it is an empty romanticism to say: "Spare us any talk about dogmas, Christology, and the Holy Spirit, or the Trinity. It is more than enough to announce God the Father and to proclaim that all men are brothers, and to live that concept without any mystical theories." Such comments seem quite plausible, but is this really the way to take into account how complex a human being is? How do we know then what fatherhood is, and what it means to be brothers and sisters. We who place our trust in these concepts, do we know why we do?

It is certain that we find in ancient cultures moving testimonies about putting a pure trust in a "Father" in heaven. But as it evolved, religious attention generally turned aside quickly from this concept to direct itself toward forces that were immediately present. When history developed, the image of humanity, and thus also the image of God, everywhere took on equivocal traits. The Greeks, as we know, called their god Zeus *father*. But for them this was not a word of trust. On the contrary, it expressed the equivocal character of God, the tragic ambiguity of the world, and its fearful aspect. When they said "Father," that meant that Zeus was like all human fathers — sometimes agreeable if he was in good humor, but basically an egoist and a disconcerting, impenetrable, and dangerous tyrant. This was exactly how they used to experience the mysterious power that governs the world — a power that pampered certain people as its favorites while it indifferently allowed others to die of hunger, to become slaves, or to waste away. The "Father" of the world as experienced in life was a reflection of the fathers of human beings — someone who was biased and in the long run disturbing.

As for the "brotherhood" that has been exhalted so enthusiasticlly in our day and that turns away from the world of fatherhood, do our own experiences reveal it to be so self-evident and so promising? The first brothers in the world, according to the Bible, were Cain and Abel, and in Roman mythology Romulus and Remus were their counterparts. Here we are concerned with a current motif, which is like a cruel parody of the hymn to brotherhood, even though it comes straight out of real life. Haven't our experiences since 1789 given new traits that are even more terrible to this parody?* Haven't they confirmed the Cain and Abel image in place of the promising meaning of the word *brotherhood*?

---

*Brotherhood here refers to *Fraternité*, one of the slogans of the French Revolution. — *Trans.*

But then, how do we know that fatherhood is something good on which we can count? How do we know if despite all appearances, God may not be playing with the world? How do we know that he loves the world with a love that does not deceive? To let us know this, God had to show himself, to topple idols, and to establish a new standard of measurement. That was realized in the Son, Jesus Christ. His whole life was immersed through prayer in the unfathomable depth of truth and goodness that is God. Only through the Son could we learn what a Father truly is. Those who criticized religion in the nineteenth century claimed that religions had been born of what was fairest in humanity that human beings had projected up to heaven in order to make a tolerable world. The truth is that when human beings set about projecting their innermost being up to heaven, what they projected was Zeus, which was a disturbing experience. The biblical Father is not a heavenly double of human fatherhood. He contributes a new aspect and is a divine critic of human fatherhood. God establishes his own standard of measurement.[8]

If it were not for Jesus, we would not know what a "Father" truly is. This becomes clear through his prayer — the prayer that belongs intrinsically to him. A Jesus who is not perpetually immersed in the Father, or who is not in permanent communication with him would be totally different from the Jesus of the Bible and the true Jesus of history. His life starts from a nucleus of prayer, and with this starting point he has understood God, the world, and human beings. To look at the world with God's glance and to live from it — this is what it means to follow Jesus. By starting with Jesus we can see what it means to live totally from the statement that God exists. Starting with

Jesus, we see what it means to accept the first tablet of the Ten Commandments as our first requirement. He gives significance to that nucleus and shows us what it is.

This gives rise, however, to a new problem. Communication with God through prayer is essential to Jesus. Prayer is what establishes him. Without it he would not be what he is. But is prayer equally essential to the Father whom Jesus invokes, so that he too would be different if he were not invoked under that name? Or does all this only touch him lightly on the surface without going deeply into him? The reply is that it becomes the Father to say "Son" just as it becomes Jesus to say "Father." Without this invocation the Father too would not be himself. Jesus has not only a contact outside himself, but as the Son he is the recipient of God's divine being. Even before the world was created, God is already the love of the Father and the Son. And if he can become our Father and the standard of measurement of all fatherhood, it is *because he is himself* a Father from all eternity. In Jesus' prayer the inner nature of God becomes visible. We see what God is like. Faith in the triune God is nothing but the explanation of what takes place in Jesus' prayer, in which the Trinity appears in all its brilliance.

What then is the Trinity? It is clear, after what has just been said, that it means a unity in duality. But where does the Third Person suddenly come in? It will be necessary for us to devote a special meditation to this question. Right now I am only offering a provisional piece of information on this matter. Unity in duality, we might say, cannot exist. This is either because its opposite — duality — persists, and there can be no real unity. Or if the two Persons come together, then the duality has to disappear. Let us try to express ourselves in a less abstract way. The Father and the Son do not become one by dissolving into one another. They stay face to face, for love is established as a face-to-face meeting, which is not suppressed. If then each of the Persons stays himself, and if they do not mutually eliminate each other, the unity cannot consist of each Person by himself but in the fruitfulness in which each of them offers himself and is himself. They are one inasmuch as their love is fruitful and goes beyond them. In the Third Person the Father and the Son give themselves to each other, and in this gift they bring it about that each of them is himself and that they are also one.

Let us go back a bit. In Jesus' prayer the Father appears in all his brightness, Jesus is recognizable as the Son, and thus a unity that is the Trinity becomes visible. Being a Christian then means participating in Jesus' prayer, entering into his form of life, that is, into his form of prayer. Being a Christian means saying with him "Father" and becoming thus a child and a son or daughter of God — of God in the unity of the Spirit who causes us to be ourselves and thus incorporates us into the unity of God. Being a Christian means looking at the world with this nucleus as a starting point, and thus becoming free, full of hope, resolute, and confident.

By this means we have returned to the departure point of our meditation. We were baptized in the name of the Father, the Son, and the Holy Spirit without knowing what it means. Today doubts attack us from all sides as to the value of this gesture. We have the impression that others took decisions for us and that they imposed them on us when, in reality, only we can take such decisions for ourselves. In this way we express our deep lack of certainty with regard to the Christian faith. We experience it as a burden rather than a grace — a burden which we may only demand by ourselves. But we forget that life also was given to us without our being asked any questions, and that with life we were given many other things. When a human being is born, not only is biological existence given to him or her but also language and a period in history with its way of thinking and its value judgments. No life is possible without a gift in advance. It is not a question of knowing whether such a gift exists but rather what it is. If baptism gives us in advance the fact of being loved by eternal love, what gift could be more precious and purer than this? The previous gift of life, in and for itself, has no meaning and can become a terrible burden. Have we the right to give life? This is uniquely defensible if life itself is defensible — if it is sustained by a hope that goes beyond all earthly horrors.[9]

When the Church only appears to be an occasional association, the previous gift of faith becomes a debatable point. But whoever is convinced that it is not a question of an association but rather the gift of a love that was waiting for us even before we began to breathe — such a person will know no task more precious than the one of preparing a human being for the gift of the love that alone justifies the gift of life. We must therefore learn again to understand above all that being a Christian is something that begins with God. It is faith in his love and it means believing that he is the Father, Son, and Holy Spirit. Only thus does the statement that he is Love have a meaning. For if he is not so in and of himself, he is not so at all. But if he is so in himself, he can only be I and You and thus be one in three Persons. Let us ask him to open our eyes so that we may understand Christian life once more by starting out with Him, and that we may understand ourselves in him anew by renewing humanity.

GOD THE CREATOR

Martin Buber in his Hasidic stories tells about the first journey of the future rabbi, Levi Yitzhak, who went to visit Rabbi Schmelke of Nikolsburg. The journey was undertaken against the wishes of his father-in-law and out of a desire to deepen his knowledge of the final realities. When he came back, his father-in-law is said to have reprimanded him in these words: "Well now, what did you learn at the rabbi's place?" And Levi Yitzhak answered: "I learned that there is a creator of the world." The old man summoned a servant and asked him: "Do you know that there is a creator of the world?" "Yes," said the servant. "Of course," exclaimed Levi Yitzhak, "everybody says so, but do people really learn about it?"[10] In this meditation let us try to "learn" a little more deeply what it means when we say God is the creator.

What does this statement mean? First of all, it means

that Christian faith is concerned with the totality of reality. It has to do with human reason. It asks a question
that concerns the whole human being. Of course, the
proofs for the existence of God have been declared out of
date for quite some time — even by theology. It is correct
that these proofs have been put forward all too often and
that their rooting in deeper problems of which we have
already spoken has not been sufficiently considered. It is
equally correct that from the viewpoint of human thought,
they have not always been correctly carried out. Finally,
we must state that the word *proof* has acquired in scien-
tific thought a meaning that it cannot certainly have in
our context. To this extent some corrections have become
necessary.

But if what we are concerned with here were totally set
aside, something would take place that would have heavy
consequences. We would remove from faith its opening to
the domain of the reason common to all human beings.
Now in places where this is the case, faith shrinks until
it is only a particular circumstance. It is no longer more
than just one of the numerous traditions of humanity —
some people have this one, others have that one. It is no
longer the truth, and has become only folklore. At one
time faith was a necessity founded on inwardness, but
now it becomes a commodity that is solicited and that no
longer brings joy to anyone. The joy of faith is linked de-
cisively to the fact of knowing that it is not just anything
but the precious pearl of truth.

All the same, the transparency of a world that reveals
its creator should be greater than ever, especially in our
own time. What formerly seemed to be inert matter we
grasp today as a form filled with spirit. As we penetrate

into the depth of the structure of solids, that is, of "mass," these depths become more and more transparent, more and more porous. "Mass" escapes us quite obviously, but the spirit reveals to us more and more triumphantly relations and structures whose harmony humiliates us and fills us with admiration.

In a conversation with friends Heisenberg expressed in a striking way the fact that another process is being developed parallel to the construction of modern physics.* It is the abandonment of a personal and positivist position that forbids physicists to ask themselves any questions about God. He shows that a knowledge of the real and of its profundity has forced physicists to interrogate the structures that bear the real. What we formerly understood under the word *God* is first of all considered in these conversations under the key term *central organization*.[11] The true content hidden behind this prudent and still tentative concept is revealed when we ask a question we can no longer avoid. Is this organization capable of asserting itself beyond the simple fact that it exists? Has this organization a quality that should be thought of in a way analogous to the way in which we think of the human person: "Can you — or can we — approach very closely the central organization of things and facts whose existence we cannot doubt at all? Can we enter a relationship with it as closely as we can with the soul of another person? . . . If you ask me this question, I shall reply yes."[12]

Setting out from this point, Heisenberg did not fear to

*Werner Carl Heisenberg (1901–   ), German physicist, winner of the Nobel prize in 1932. — *Trans.*

link the issue of the *central organization* to the issue of the *compass* whose direction we should follow if we are seeking a pathway through life.[13] In fact, to speak of the central organization brings us back again to something like a compass, to a requirement, to a point of reference. It is then logical that Heisenberg does not draw back even before the quite concrete consequences that certainly lead him far beyond his point of departure — the observation of order in the world, namely, the fact that Christian faith encourages us to submit to that central organization. "Once the magnetic attraction that has guided this compass comes to a halt — and it is clear that such an attraction can only arise for the central organization — I fear that dreadful things may take place, things that go beyond even the concentration camps and the atomic bombs."[14]

We have gone ahead of ourselves, however, at this point. Christian faith is not against reason, but protects reason. Only a little while ago people readily complained that the faith was hostile to progress and cultivated an unhealthful resentment against technology. In our own day, when it is now fashionable to doubt the blessings of technology, a very different complaint is heard. With its slogan "master the earth" and its policy of banishing the old gods from the world, the Christian faith is accused of having produced humanity's desire for a limitless dominion and exploitation of the earth. The Church is thus said to have caused the curse of technology. Let us leave aside the problem of what the Christians' share of blame may be in all the minor aspects of this or that sphere. In both of these accusations, however, we are mistaken as to the direction of the faith. Certainly, our faith places the world in the hands of human beings, and to this extent it has

contributed to the coming of modern times. But it has always linked the issue of human dominion over the world
with the issue of divine creation and the significance of
that creation. Our faith allows us to devote ourselves to
research and technical matters because it interprets the
rationality and order of the world as a function of human
beings. But Christianity is deeply opposed to the concentration of our minds on the solely practical and useful.
It summons human beings to go beyond their own immediate interests and seek the essence of things. It protects
a kind of reasoning that is perceptive and opposes the use
of a purely instrumental kind of reasoning.

At the same time another point is becoming clear. In
our belief in divine creation we are not concerned about a
mere theory nor about the remote past when the world
was born. We are concerned about the present and about
the correct posture we should assume with regard to reality. For Christian faith in creation, it is decisive that the
Creator and the Savior, the God of the beginning and the
God of the end should be one and the same God. Wherever
this unity is broken, heresy is born and the faith is
shattered in its basic aspect. This temptation is as old as
the world, although the forms under which it now appears
make it seem brand-new. Early in the history of the Church,
Marcion, who was from Asia Minor, expressed this idea
for the first time in a fascinating way.* He did not accept

---

*Marcion, a heretical leader, was born at Sinope in Pontus and
died about 160. He rejected the Old Testament as the revelation
of a cruel God who was not the God of Jesus. Many of his fol-
lowers merged with the Manichaean heretics in the third century. — *Trans.*

the unity between Jesus and the God of the Old Testament that had been affirmed by the majority of the Church. Marcion objected that the New Testament expressly stated that the Jews did not know the father of Jesus Christ, and that they did not know his God. Therefore the God of the Old Testament could not be the God of Jesus Christ. Jesus was said to have contributed a truly new God, one unknown up to that time, who had nothing in common with the jealous, angry, and vengeful God of the Old Covenant. Jesus' God — *his own God* — is only love, forgivness, and joy; his God no longer threatens; he is in every respect hope and forgiveness; he is solely a "good God." According to Marcion, Jesus came to free humanity from the old God's law and from the old God himself, and to place it in the hands of the merciful God who appeared in Jesus Christ himself. This slander against the old God, as Marcion perceived him to be, was at the same time a slander against God's "failed" creation. It was a revolt against creation and in favor of a new world.[15]

Whoever follows attentively the spiritual evolution of our period can attest to the fact that we may really speak of a present day return of Marcion's concepts in more than one sense. Of course, there are differences, and these differences usually draw the attention of a superficial observer. We can point out that Marcion's rejection of creation led him to an almost neurotic hatred of the body — something that appears quite remote from us today. Perhaps such an attitude would have been appropriate in the "darkness of the Middle Ages." According to this view, most of the Church inherited this medieval idea, which we are overcoming today. But now let's ask ourselves if people in the Middle Ages could have built such cathedrals and

THE GOD OF JESUS CHRIST

composed music if there did not exist in them a deep love
of creation, of things, and of the human body? This type
of argument, however, does not bring us to the essential
point. For in fact, it was the rejection of the creator and
his creation that linked Marcion to the important tendency
known as gnosis. From it arose both an ascetical scorn for
the human body and a cynical kind of debauchery, which
is really only a form of hatred for the body, for humanity,
and for the world. The two trends that on the surface seem
far apart from each other are closely associated. The basic
attitudes they presuppose are based on one another. In the
false asceticism that is hostile to creation, the body is regarded as nothing more than a package of dirty linen
worthy only of contempt, and even of mistreatment. In the
same way deliberate debauchery is based on the fact that
the living body (*Leib*) is reduced to a simple anatomical
body (*Körper*), that is, to just an object. To exclude the
body from the moral domain and the responsibility of the
spirit means to exclude it from what is human in humanity
and from the dignity of the spirit. The body becomes a
mere object or thing, and at the same time the lives of
human beings themselves lose all value and become vul-
gar. In the final analysis, haven't we met up with Marcion
by starting out from a different point of view? And are
there not also in theology subtle forms of a similar rejection
of the body from the domain of the human, and of a similar
materialization and a similar scorn connected with it? Do
we not find ourselves in a similar situation where God no
longer has anything in common with the human body? According to such a theology, every attempt to fathom the
bodily in connection with Jesus, who was born of the
Virgin, and in connection with a belief in the Resurrection

— 36 —

of the Lord is rejected as an unreasonable form of naïveté.

Such a view point also rejects with many scrowls the possibility that God can make himself so concrete and so material.

We have not yet grasped, however, the full import of such a viewpoint. If human beings scorn their bodies — through asceticism or through debauchery — they scorn themselves. Both an asceticism that is hostile to creation and debauchery cause human beings to have to hate the life that is theirs — to hate themselves and reality in all its aspects. That is where the explosive political force of these two positions is located. Human beings feeling themselves dishonored, want to destroy everything having to do with the ignominious prison of the body as well as the world in order to run away from this humiliation. Their outbursts against the other world rest on a hatred of creation and the God who must reply for all this. And so gnosis has become — for the first time in the history of the human spirit — an ideology of total revolution.[16] It is no longer a question of political and social struggles over power, such as we have always known, but something more basic: anger in the face of reality itself, which human beings have learned to hate as a result of the ups and downs of their existence. By despising their bodies, human beings split up, beginning with the very root of their being, which no longer seems to them created but "subsisting," and thus something to destroy. In their revolutionary ideologies Marx and Marcion are very close to each other. It is because revolution, starting as a political means, becomes a religious idol. Then there is no longer any question of struggle between this or that political concept, but a question of different gods. It becomes a question of a revolt against

THE GOD OF JESUS CHRIST

reality itself which as a subsisting reality must be trodden underfoot to make way for a totally new universe. And for that reason a discussion about judgments of ethical values will never be a dispute over morality. It will always be over Being itself and becomes a metaphysical quarrel. When the existence of the family, fatherhood, and motherhood are defamed as if they were obstacles to liberty; when respect, obedience, fidelity, patience, goodness, and trust are qualified as inventions of the ruling classes; when we teach our children that hatred, distrust, and disobedience are true virtues for human beings who are liberating themselves — then the Creator and his creation are themselves placed in question. All of creation would then be replaced by another world that human beings construct for themselves. In the logic of this hypothesis of departure, only hatred can in the end be the pathway to love, but this logic is based on a preliminary condition — the antilogic of the destruction of ourselves. For when everything real is slandered and when the Creator is vilified, human beings are cutting out their own roots. At a much lower level we begin to perceive this idea very concretely — the problems of the environment demonstrate to us that human beings cannot live in contradiction with the earth because they must live from the earth. But we do not always wish to agree that this is valid for reality in all its aspects.

What has just been said brings out little by little our previous statements. Without further explanation but stressing Heisenberg we say: Creation is not only a matter of theoretical reasoning, of contemplation, and of surprise, but it is also a "compass."[17] The Ancients spoke about the natural law. Today the concept of the natural law is ridiculed, and in this area there has certainly been much abuse.

All the same its essential point remains as follows: There is law "by reason of nature," which is directed by creation and which at the same time makes possible the law of nations beyond the frontiers of the different nation-states. There is what is law by nature and that precedes our law-giving in such a way that, among all the things human beings invent, not everything can be "just" by a long shot. There can be laws that, although laws, are still not "justice," but injustice. Nature itself, because it has been created, is a source of law. It points out the limits that should not be crossed. Events of immediate significance in this respect are obvious. If we make the murder of an innocent life a right, we are transforming what is unjust into what is just. If the law no longer protects human life, we may question it as law. To affirm this point does not mean to want to impose on others a specifically Christian morality in a pluralist society. It is a question of "humanity," of what is human in human beings, which cannot make crushing creation a liberation, unless we greatly delude ourselves. The passionate character of the dispute over this issue is due to the depth of the problem. Are human beings only free if they remove the chains that bind them to creation and leave creation behind them like something that enslaves them? Rather are not human beings denying themselves by this same act? It is at this level that, in the last instance, the fight is joined so that human beings may be truly human. Christians cannot dispense themselves from assuming it by saying that their morality in any case is not shared by others. For then we would be mistaking the scope of the question as well as the scope of the Christian situation, which is more than a group ethic. It is a responsibility with regard to humanity in its entire being.

This is precisely a result of the fact that humanity's liberator is none other than the Creator.

A new and significant aspect of the situation of today's humanity now appears. In these anxious efforts to block the path of new human life in the most silent and certain way possible, isn't there a deep fear of the future? In this fear there seem to be two different elements. On the one hand, this fear certainly is due to the fact that the gift of of life no longer seems to have meaning to us because the meaning of the gift has slowly disappeared. We recognize in it despair over our own lives, which does not want to impose on others the dark highway of humanity. On the other hand, there is also — quite obviously and quite frankly — a fear of competition and a fear of the restrictions that another life would certainly become for us. The other person — the one who is to come — becomes a danger. True love is a death, an obliteration of oneself before and for another. But we do not desire death. We wish to remain ourselves and to consume our lives with the least amount of sharing and disturbance possible for ourselves. We do not perceive, and do not wish to perceive, that we are really destroying our own future by such a thirst for life that as a result our own lives fall into the hands of death.

At the same time a final aspect appears to us: Trust in God the Creator means also trust in the God of conscience. Because he is the Creator, he is close to each of us in our conscience. In our trust in our own conscience is manifest the very personal content of our profession of faith in creation. Conscience is above the law: It distinguishes between the just law and the unjust law. Conscience is the priority of the truth; that is, it is not a fantastic principle but an expression of faith in the secret complicity between human beings and the truth. Through our consciences we are parties to the truth. Thus, our conscience provokes us at the same time to go ever further in our search for the truth.

I believe in God the Creator. Let us pray to him that we "learn" what this really means.

JOB AND HIS QUESTION

The image of God is humanity. The God of the Old Testament does not tolerate any other image. In the Holy of Holies of the Temple no statue of God arose as in the temples of other peoples, but only an empty throne containing the tablets of his holy word and a jar filled with manna.[18] Such is his image: an empty throne reflecting his sovereignty and infinite power; his word, which is the expression of his holiness that wishes to live in humanity; and his bread, which is the symbol of his power over creation and history, the symbol of his kindness that sustains the creatures for whom he has made a habitable world. All this reflects human beings. They should be God's throne and the dwelling place of his word; they live from the kindness of creation and from him who made it. Human beings alone are the image of God.

When we look at matters more closely, we may be gripped by a feeling of anxiety. Of course, there still occur from time to time — God be praised! — blessed moments when something of God appears to us in human beings. In the great works of art that human beings have received during their history, we have a presentiment of some of God's creative imagination, of his creative Spirit, of his eternal Beauty that exceeds all words and all the calculations of logic. Even more profoundly do we experience in the kindness of a human being who is good without knowing why, something of God himself. A witness told me one day about a group of young Asian girls who, after experiencing all kinds of misfortunes, were taken in and cared for by some nuns. Those young girls spoke to the sisters as if they were speaking to God for, as they said, a human being is not capable of such kindness.

Thus an openness to God exists in human beings — thanks be God! But how often is our experience of life more strongly characterized by just the opposite view. Human beings seem, throughout their history, to have given proofs of the existence of a demon — or at least of an equivocal being — rather than of the existence of a kindly God. Human beings invalidate the God confirmed by creation. This is perhaps the true reason that proofs for the existence of God in the end remain always in vain. Humanity disfigures what shines like a light through the elements of creation. There is no need to recall the dreadful names of Nero, Hitler, and Stalin. It's enough to think of our own experiences with people just like us and with ourselves. In addition to the faults of human beings and the darkness to which they give rise, there is the baffling suffering of the innocent — a most terrible accusation against God which from Job to Dostoevsky and Auschwitz rises in a chorus of ever more disturbing outcries. Job cannot accept the excuse for God by means of which his friends attempt to explain away Job's suffering. This excuse, however, is identical with the wisdom of Israel up to that time, which regarded suffering as a punishment for sin and prosperity as a reward for virtue. In this way the world seems to be a system of rewards and punishments according to a strict form of justice, even though we are not always in a position to know the reasons for such a system. Job rebelled with all the passion of an innocent, tortured man against such an image of God. His experience had been quite different:

> Both the innocent and the wicked he destroys. When the scourge slays suddenly, he laughs at the despair of the innocent. The earth is given into the hands of the wicked; he covers the face of its judges. If it is not he, who then is it? (Job 9: 22–24).

To the magnificent song trust that knows itself to be in safety with an all-present God (Psalm 138),[19] Job opposes a quite opposite experience:

> But if I go to the east, he is not there; or to the west, I cannot perceive him; where the north enfolds him, I behold him not; by the south he is veiled, and I see him not (Job 23: 8–9).

The original joy of living is broken by this experience:

Why then did you bring me forth from the womb? I should have died and no eye have seen me (Job 10: 18).

Behind Job's outcry rise up today the millions of nameless persons who passed into the gas chambers at Auschwitz and into the prisons of the dictatorships of the left and the right. Where is your God? The accusers cry this out more and more loudly. Of course, there is often in such outbursts more cynicism than true respect for the horror of human suffering. But the accusation is correct. Where are you then, O God? Who are you to be silent?

Only God himself can reply, and he has not yet done so in a definitive way. He has not done so in such a way that we can place his response on the table and redo our calculations. But he has not been completely silent either. Indeed, his final word has not been spoken. In the Resurrection of Jesus he has only made a beginning. This is the way he always goes about things: He demands of human beings not only their intelligence but also their hearts and their very selves. In the case of Job, this is how things start out: God himself took part in the debate, and did not place himself on the side of his defenders. He rejected as blasphemy an explanation that made of him the cruel and rigorous executor of a false justice that was minutely calculated. The outcries of Job did not offend him; instead, he was offended by the harshness of those who depicted the countenance of God as a dreadful mechanism for vengeance. But Job received no explanations. He was only able to become aware of his own smallness and of the poorness of the perspective from which he looked at the world. He learned how to quiet down, how to be silent, and to have hope. His heart was set adrift — nothing more.

This humility of silence should be of concern to us also as a first step toward wisdom.

Moreover, it is striking to note that accusations against God come only from a minimal portion of those who suffer in the world — to a much larger degree they come from satisfied spectators who have never suffered. For those who suffer have learned to see. Each individual has his or her own relationship with God, and we cannot count human beings quantitatively as if they were some kind of commodity. The praises of God come in this world from the furnaces of those who suffer; the account of the three young men in the fiery furnace contains a truth that is more profound than learned treatises.[20]

The response to Job was only a beginning — a hesitating anticipation of the response that God gave in pledging his own Son the cross and the Resurrection of Jesus Christ. In this instance also nothing can be verified in a qualitative manner. God's response was not an explanation but an action. The response was an act of compassion — it was not like a simple act of feeling, but it was a reality. The compassion of God took on flesh. We know it in the scourging, the crowning with thorns, the crucifixion, and the tomb. God entered into our suffering. What this means and what it can mean, let us learn from the great pictures of the crucified Christ or from the Pietàs where the Mother mourns her dead son. In such works of art, suffering has been transformed for human beings who have learned that God himself dwells at the heart of their sufferings and that through their wounds they have become one with him. Let us not speak of consolation. For such an experience is a source of love for those who suffer, including such examples as Francis of Assisi and Elizabeth of Hungary.

The crucified Christ has not removed suffering from the world, but by his cross he has changed human beings and turned their hearts towards their suffering sisters and brothers. By his cross he has strengthened and purified both those who suffer and those who feel sorrow for them. From Christ comes that "respect of what is beneath us"* that is lacking in pagan humanism and that dies as soon as faith in the crucified Christ comes to an end. Are we not slowly beginning to understand — with all the problems of our Social Security systems — that there are some things we cannot pay for? Are we not slowly realizing, as a result of changes going on today, the transformation that faith used to confer in the past, which was more than an empty "consolation"?

We must now take a step forward. The cross did not remain God's final word in Jesus Christ. The tomb did not keep possession of Jesus. He arose again and spoke to us through the risen God. The rich voluptuary in hell asked if Lazarus might receive permission to appear to the rich man's brothers to warn them about their brother's dreadful fate. If someone would rise up from the dead, he claimed, they would believe (Luke 16: 27-31). Well, for us the true Lazarus has already come. He is here and tells us that our life is not all. There is eternity. To speak about such things today, even in theological circles, is quite old-fashioned. To speak about the world beyond seems like a flight from our world here below. Yes, but if it's the truth? Can we then bypass it? Can we abolish it under the pretext that it is just a form of consolation? Isn't this what gives to life its importance, its freedom, and its hope?

*Quotation from Wilhelm Wolfgang von Goethe. — *Trans.*

Humanity is the image of God. This image is presented to us, however, with many distortions. And so this statement is perfectly applied only to Jesus Christ who is the restored image of God. But what God do we see? On the basis of a misunderstood theology, many derived from it a quite false image — the image of a cruel God who demands the death of his own Son. They have read in it the image of the friends of Job, and have turned away in fright from that God. But the very opposite is true: The God of the Bible demanded no human sacrifice. In the history of religions where he appeared, human sacrifice came to an end. Before Abraham could lay a hand on Isaac, a divine intervention prevented him, and a goat took the child's place. Here is where devotion to Yahweh began: The sacrifice of the first-born demanded by Abraham's traditional religion was replaced by his obedience and his faith. What replaced Isaac in an external way — the goat — was only an expression of that deeper happening in which it was not a question of replacing Isaac but of going right to the basic issue.[21] For the God of Israel human sacrifice was an abomination. Moloch, the god of human sacrifices, was the very essence of the false gods which the belief of Yahweh opposed.[22] For the God of Israel the death of a human being was not a sacrificial offering but his life. Irenaeus of Lyons* expressed this in his wonderful formula: *Gloria Dei homo vivens* (The glory of God is a live human being). This is the kind of human sacrifice God requested.[23]

If this is so, what is the meaning of the cross of the

---

*Irenaeus (ca. 140–ca. 202), early Church father and bishop of Lyons. Born in Asia Minor, he was a vigorous opponent of Gnosticism. — *Trans.*

Lord? It is a form of the love that has totally taken hold of humanity and as a result has also descended into the sin and death of humanity. Thus this love has become a "sacrifice": a love without limits that has taken up humanity — a lost sheep — onto his shoulders and brought it back to the Father through the night of sin. Ever since then there has been a new way of suffering that is not a curse but a love that transforms the world.

CHAPTER 2

Jesus Christ

HE CAME DOWN
FROM HEAVEN

In its christological articles the Nicene Creed[1] presents the Lord first of all as "the only Son of God, eternally begotten of the Father, God from God, Light from Light, true God from true God, begotten not made, one in Being with the Father. Through him all things were made." By its affirmation the Creed remains in the domain of what preceded our world. The connection with the earthly person of Jesus is made in these words: "For us men and for our salvation he came down from heaven."

The new German translation has avoided the expression *came down,* surely in the thought that such an expression imposes considerable problems of comprehension for present-day people. On two points it is inevitable that this expression shocks us. First of all, the question is raised whether God makes himself dependent on human beings? Can an accidental become the basis of the Eternal? Can it be that the basis of God and of divine action is not always God himself? Has God the possibility — has he even the right to act — for someone other than God? Or could it be that God then is acting in a divine manner, that is, for the sake of God, even when he is acting for humanity?

There is another cause for scandal, however, that is no less profound but more immediate: are we not presupposing a vision of the world in three stages as it appears in mythology? Are we not presupposing that God lives high above the clouds while human beings live below and that our earth is a soil of creation to which God must descend to put the universe back in order again?

In the background other questions arise that go even further and at the same time eliminate the preceding ones on more than one count. We do not like the concept of someone coming down to another person. We don't want any "condescension." We want equality. The Scriptural expression *deposuit potentes de sede* (He has thrown down the mighty from their thrones) agrees with us more than *descendit de coelis,* although both go together. For a God who comes down is precisely one who dethrones the mighty and raises up to the rank of the first those who were previously last. But we prefer to take the responsibility on ourselves for throwing down the mighty without divine intervention. A view of the world in which there is no longer high or low, that is, a world in every respect equal to itself and without solid points of support is not just an exterior view. It corresponds at the same time to a new attitude toward reality, which consists of considering the view of a high and a low as an illusion. It is an attitude that wants to dethrone everything on high with a view to the equality, freedom, and dignity of human beings. In fact, we can say that if God came down and if he is now below, what was below is now on high. Therefore, the old distinction between high and low no longer exists. And the view of the world and humanity has changed. But it has changed precisely because of the God who came down.

First and foremost then, the statement that he *came down* remains. It cannot be reduced or replaced. What it amounts to is an affirmation that the greatness, glory, and lordship of God and of Jesus Christ exist as well as the unconditional supremacy of God's Word, love, and power. The high point exists, which is God. The second article of faith does not abolish the first one. Even in the most extreme descent, even in the supreme humiliation and the most secret kind of life, God remains the true high point. Before considering the story of salvation, we forcefully posit the basic affirmation that God exists. At first, we must recall to mind the intangible supremacy of the One from whom everything proceeds. If we do not see the coming down of God, it loses at the same time its greatness. It is lost in the general indifference of pointless circular movements of things indefinitely like themselves. If we do not see it, not only are the drama of history and the drama of the human condition without interest and meaning but human beings also do not emerge from it enlarged but diminished. Humanity is no longer itself a high point of the world but one of the games in which the world tries out its own possibilities. Humanity is "an animal that has not yet been established," according to Nietzsche.

Whoever wishes to understand Jesus' coming down should first of all grasp the mystery of the high point suggested by the expression *heaven*. The mystery of the burning bush is placed at the beginning — the power that forces our respect and fixes the scales of value. But the fire of the burning bush was not a universal fire in the meaning of Stoical philosophy. From it emerged a voice proclaiming that God had heard the groans of his people reduced to slavery, Israel's cry of distress. This fire was itself the coming down of a God who was on the side of an unfortunate people. We can therefore give a first result of our reflections. It was not a question of coming down in space from a higher stage of the world to an inferior stage, but it was a question of something much deeper, which ought to be symbolized in a dramatic action. This action will show the movement of the divine Being as it passed into the being of humanity; even further, the movement went from majesty to the cross, and went to the last who as a result became the first. We can only begin to perceive the depth of the meaning this expression *coming down* by following its long history in the writings of the Old and New Testaments. At first, it was just a tiny streamlet, which later turned into a river that gathered together more and more streams and tributaries. In the account of the Tower of Babel, the coming down of God appeared first like an angry descent, and it was followed in the story of the burning bush by a new coming down full of compassion and love.

In this meditation I would like to choose two representative passages — one from the Old Testament and the other from the New Testament — that take on a special meaning in the history of the theme of God's coming down, even though neither passage makes use of this term.

1. The Animals and the Son of Man in Chapter 7 of Daniel

We have today good reason to date the Book of Daniel in its present form to 167 to 163 B.C., that is, to a time when Israel's faith was harshly persecuted by the Hellenistic king, Antiochus IV Epiphanes. Through extreme tribulations the faith of God's people and its historical hope seemed to have definitively reached a dead end. As a result, however, the prophet had a new vision of history in its totality.

After the exile, Israel had not known its long-awaited greatness. It had stayed a dependent and poor nation and failed to regain its autonomy. In place of the new and magnificent temple that Ezechial had predicted, Israel had only succeeded in erecting with difficulty a poor substitute, which was far below the magnificence of the first temple. The pilgrimage of the peoples to Israel had changed nothing in this situation. On the contrary, Israel itself in its distress was beginning to be scattered among other nations. The triumph of Alexander the Great and his successors had definitely reduced to nothing every hope of improvement. Skepticism appeared in Israel. After the dramatic battle with God Job had dared to carry out, Koheleth or the preacher in Ecclesiastes was nothing but a weary resignation. Everything was in vain; there was nothing to do except take out of life what was left in it. Finally, an enlightened form of Greek rationalism pervaded the land triumphantly, filling the empty space that opened up voluntarily for this universal civilization. It brought with it the legitimation of power and success. Only the person who accepted freedom and the vast spiritual horizons of Greece could still have opportunities. The path of progress fol-

lowed by history was clear. Circumcision, which was regarded as a repugnant pagan rite, disappeared. Gymnasiums
were built as the new center of a humanistic civilization.
The gods of an enlightened Greek rationalism more and
more took the place of Yahweh.

In this situation Antiochus IV Epiphanes became in the
eyes of the rare believers in Israel — a ridiculous minority
that had not yet accepted progress — the symbol par ex-
cellance of the powers in history that were hostile to
God. Daniel called him a little horn (Chapters 7 and 8)
who spoke arrogantly. But what was revolting was the fact
that such a "little horn" could turn the God of Israel into
ridicule and trample Israel's faith beneath his feet. Never-
theless, in the mind of the seer the trials of that time were
inserted into a total movement. That horn belonged to the
fourth empire; for the history of the world was dominated
in succession by four beasts that arose from the sea. Finally,
the earth was restored to the hands of one who comes from
on high and who was like a "Son of man." Everything was
in this opposition: The powers that up to that time had
ruled over the earth were beasts coming from below —
from the sea, which was a symbol of what was disturbing,
dangerous, and evil. In confrontation with them was the
man — and Israel with him. The man came from on high,
from the divine space. For the seer, history thus reproduced
to a certain degree the unfolding of the creation of the
world as represented to us in the account in Genesis. At
first beasts inhabited the earth. But in the end, humanity
was destined to reign over the world after God had mas-
tered the power of chaos and fixed limits to the sea. In
the middle of the trials of his time, Daniel made the following affirmation: Be fearless. Even if the beasts are now

in power, history will finally fulfill the promise of creation.[2]

In the book of Daniel an oppressed Israel expressed its hope of seeing the end of the sacriligious power of the Hellenistic empires and called them beasts that came out of the depths. The image of the Son of man in the Book of Daniel has become one of the basic conditions of the profession of faith, which speaks of the coming down of the incarnate God in the Son of man, Jesus Christ. It was a part of the background that gave meaning to the phrase in our Creed of which we have been speaking. At the same time that phrase meant that in opposition to the one who came from below — the bestial power whose arrogant brutality was destroying the world — was the "man" who came from on high. It was this opposition that comprised his powerlessness as well as his victory. His lack of power was due to the fact that man was not a beast, nor did he have a beast's devouring mouth, iron tusks, metal claws, and horns that caused a dreadful noise. In confrontation with such warlike equipment, man was like one abandoned and doomed. But this clear image had also its victory, and in the end man was indeed the king of the animals, which he was to master with a hidden power that had been given power belonged to him, and at the same time that "power" to him — the power of the spirit and the heart. Finally, power belonged to him, and at the same time that "power" had been changed.

Jesus, the Son of God, came as a man among the beasts. In the weakness of his humanity he established divine sovereignty. Precisely, by the sign of his weakness that was opposed to brutality, he incarnated divine greatness. He came among the beasts without becoming himself a beast and without using their methods. And he let himself be devoured, but in that way he triumphed over them. For what was an apparent defeat was a victory. There was no bestial element in this victory. There was a love that went to the very end (John 13:1). In him humanity was renewed.

Jesus came among beasts under a human form. That meant that he also sought those who were with him, who placed themselves on his side, who placed their trust in the power of the Man from on high and thus allowed themselves to be saved.

2.   The Coming Down From Heaven as a Spiritual Event

In Chapter 10 of the Epistle to the Hebrews we find one of the most profound interpretations of the coming down of the Son — an interpretation from which any reference of a spatial nature had disappeared so that its personal and spiritual content appears fully illuminated. The author of the Epistle takes up again his major concept: the sacrifice of animals is not appropriate for reestablishing the relationship between God and humanity. He then continues: "Therefore, in coming into the world he [Christ] says, 'Sacrifice and oblation thou wouldst not, but a body thou hast fitted to me: In holocausts and sin-offerings thou hast had no pleasure. Then said I, 'Behold I come — (in the head of the book it is written of me) — to do thy will, O God' " (Heb. 10: 5–9; Ps 39: 7–9). By returning to a psalm, which is interpreted as the prayer of Jesus as he enters the world, the Epistle gives a true theology of the Incarnation in which there is no question about a universe in stages. The "coming down" and the "entrance" are rather considered as methods of prayer — prayer being understood here as a real event, like the taking possession of all existence, which in prayer starts up and throws off all restraint. The entrance of Christ into the cosmos is therefore interpreted here as a voluntary event in conformity with the Word and like a concrete accomplishment of this direction of thought and faith that found expression in the religious fervor of various psalms.

Let us now consider more closely the text of the psalm and its transformation in the New Testament. What does the psalm say? It is the thanksgiving of one whom God has awakened from among the dead.[3] The person saying the prayer, however, does not thank God by sacrificing an animal. Placing himself in the line of the prophetical tradition, he is aware of this fact: "Sacrifice or oblation you wished not, but ears open to obedience you gave me" (Ps. 39: 7–9). This means that God does not want material gifts but the ear of the person who is praying: his hearing, his obedience, and as a result of these things, the man himself. This is what true thanksgiving consists of, a thanksgiving agreeable to God: to enter into the will of God.

For the Epistle of the Hebrews, these words of the psalm reveal the dialogue between the Father and the Son that is the Incarnation. The Incarnation can be recognized thus as a spiritual event within the Trinity. The epistle has only replaced a *single* word as a result of the illumination of the Fulfillment: In place of references to the person's ear and sense of hearing we find the body — ". . . a body thou has fitted to me." This word *body* signifies the human condition itself, the union with human nature.

Obedience takes on flesh. In its highest realization it is no longer only just the sense of hearing but the Incarnation. The theology of the word becomes the theology of the Incarnation. The gift of the Son to the Father extends beyond the dialogue within the Trinity: It becomes the acceptance of creation summed up in humanity — and thus it becomes the gift of this creation. This body, or more precisely the humanity of Jesus, is the product of obedience, the fruit of the response of love of the Son. At the same time it is a prayer that has become concrete. The humanity of Jesus, in this sense, is already a factual state that is totally spiritual and "divine" from its very beginning.

If we consider all this, it is obvious that there exists a deep internal link between the humiliation of the Incarnation and even the Crucifixion on the one hand, and the mystery of the Son on the other hand. The very nature of the Son is to give himself freely and to take himself back freely. Son, if translated into the terms of a creature, means one who "humbled himself, becoming obedient to death, even to death on a cross" (Phil. 2:8). Thus the passage again comes down from the height of the mystery to penetrate within us. We do not become God by making ourselves independent of him or by living autonomously without any limits on our total emancipation — such attempts fail by reason of their internal contradiction and their character of radical opposition to the truth. But we become God by participating in the very gestures of the Son. We do so by becoming "children" and "sons," that is, by letting the dialogue we are carrying on with the Father penetrate into the flesh of our daily lives: ". . . a body thou has fitted to me."

Our salvation is in becoming "the Body of Christ," that is, like Christ himself: by agreeing each day to receive ourselves from him; by offering ourselves again each day to him; by giving each day to him our body as an occasion for the Word. We become God by walking after him in a motion that both comes down and goes up. All of this is contained in that simple phrase "he came down from heaven." It is a question of Christ, and also of ourselves. To speak of such a profession of faith cannot exhaust it. It sends us back from the Word to the body; for only in the motion of the Word to the body and from the body to the Word can we truly assimilate it.

AND BECAME MAN

The Incarnation of God is the central article of the faith of the Christian Creed. Around it has revolved for centuries the thought of the theologians who in its light have tried to grasp something about the mystery of God and humanity. These great and deep questions will not be asked in this book. We only wish to discover, so to speak, a theological secondary road in an attempt to understand what is great and distant by starting from what is near and simple, and from what affects our lives. The following reflection should help us in this effort. We can consider the human situation by beginning with its essential elements, that is, the spirit and the body, the Creator and the creature, the individual and society. But beyond these great structures that embrace everything and are inserted into everything, we can also consider this fact: The individual has never had in an instant a clear and global vision of his or her life. For the individual life also stretches out into time, and only the totality of this temporal course in the end constitutes a human being. In such a temporal situation the specifically human link is effective between the biological and the spiritual, for time is characterized for the human being by a biological unfolding of infancy, maturity, old age, and death. Human life is fashioned in these biological stages. The religious devotion of the Middle Ages and early modern times, thinking about the humanity of Jesus, became attached by preference to this reality. It spoke about the "mysteries of the life of Jesus" and meant the different phases of the Savior's historical and earthly journey.[4] Contemplation — and painting that resulted from it — lovingly delved into the periods of Jesus' earthly life in an effort to approach more closely the Unmeasurable that we confess when we say: "the Son of God became man." Would it be absolutely impossible to try to find such a path again? Let's take a few steps tentatively — it is not possible to do more than that — and let's think about what it means that Jesus experienced our human situation in the various phases of childhood, maturity, and death.

1. The Childhood of Jesus

Jesus became a child. What does it mean to be a child?[5] First of all, it means being in submission, dependence, and need — and depending on others. As a child, Jesus did not come only from God but also from other human beings. He was born in the bosom of woman from whom he received flesh and blood, the beating of his heart, gestures, and language. He received his life from another person. To have received thus what is his from others has nothing purely biological about it. It means that Jesus also received the forms of thought and the concepts of human beings who existed before him, especially the concepts of his mother, and that his human soul was filled with them. It means that along with the heritage of his ancestors he took up again the entire distance traveled up to that time and which from Mary went back to Abraham and finally to Adam. He took upon himself the weight of this history, which he lived and endured in order to transform all refusals and all deviations into a totally pure yes: "For the Son of God, Jesus Christ, who was preached among us by you . . . was not now 'Yes' and 'No', but only 'Yes' was in him" (2 Cor. 1:19).

It is striking to see how Jesus himself accorded a privileged place to childhood in the human condition: "Amen I say to you, unless you turn and become like little children, you will not enter into the kingdom of heaven" (Matt. 18:3). Being a child was thus for Jesus not a passing stage of human life that would result from its biological destiny and as a result would be wiped out without leaving any traces. In childhood, the proper sense of our human situation is realized so well that whoever has lost the essence of childhood is also lost. From this we might humanly think that the childhood of Jesus, as he recalled it, must have been particularly happy so that it remained precious to him to the extent that he considered it the purest way of being a human being. We might also learn to respect the child who as a human being without protection calls out to our love. But above all the following question is imperative: What constitutes the essence of childhood that Jesus considered so irreplaceable? For it is clear that it is not a question of a romantic glorification of children nor of a moral judgment but that it is a question of something deeper.

In the first place it is necessary for us to recall that the main title of Jesus' theological nobility is "the Son." To what degree was this designation linguistically prefigured by the way in which Jesus offered himself? However we may settle this question, there is no doubt that it is an attempt to sum up in a word the general impression of his life. The direction of his life, his origin, and his endpoint all had as their name Abba, that is, Daddy. He knew he was never alone. Up to his last outcry on the cross, he was entirely turned toward the Other, toward the one he called his Father. This is what has made it possible that his true title of nobility is finally neither king nor lord nor any other title of power, but a word that we might easily translate as "child." We can therefore say that, if childhood occupies such prominence in Jesus' preaching, it is because childhood was in close contact with this most personal mystery, his sonship. His highest dignity, which referred back to his divinity, in the end was not a power possessed for its own sake. It consisted of being directed toward the Other — toward God the

Father. Joachim Jeremias said quite correctly that to be a child in the sense in which Jesus understood it meant learning how to say Father.[6]

Only by linking all of this to Jesus and to his being a Son can we measure the immense strength that dwells in this word Father. We rediscover everything we had already encountered in our own thoughts about the triune God, who is the Creator. Humanity wishes to become God and should do so. But every time that — as happened during the eternal dialogue with the serpent in Paradise — humanity has tried to attain this goal by liberating itself from God's guardianship and from his creation in order to rely only on itself and to establish itself by itself, every time that it has become totally adult and completely emancipated, and every time it has totally rejected childhood as a state in life, humanity has emerged into nothingness because it has gone against its own truth, which is a state of dependency. Only by preserving what is most essential to childhood and to the existence of a son, as was first experienced by Jesus, does humanity enter with the Son into the divine state.

We have said nothing in all this except what is very general. Another aspect of what Jesus understood by childhood was seen in his glorification of the poor: "Blessed are you poor, for yours is the kingdom of God" (Luke 6:20). In this passage the poor have taken the place of the children. Here also there was no question of making poverty something romantic nor of forming moral judgments about the poor and the rich on an individual basis. It was a question about the very depths of the human situation. In poverty there appears something of what constitutes childhood: A child possesses nothing of his own. He receives things from others, and precisely by not possessing either power or property for himself he is free. He has as yet no social possessions to smother his personality like a mask. Goods and power are the two great temptations of human beings, who become prisoners of their property and abandon their souls to it. Human beings who are incapable because of their possessions of staying poor in their innermost being — even if they know that the world is in the hand of God and not in their own hands — have lost the childhood without which no one can enter into the kingdom.

In this connection Stylianos Harkianakis drew attention to the fact that Plato in his dialogue *Timaeus* reported an ironic judgment of a non-Greek who characterized the Greeks as eternal children [*aei paides*]. Plato saw no reproach in this but rather a praise for the Greek temperament:

> It is in any case certain that the Greeks wanted to be a people of philosophers and not technocrats — thus a nation of eternal children who saw amazement as the noblest state of human existence. Only in this way can we explain the important fact that the Greeks made no practical use of their countless discoveries.[7]

But in this reference to the discreet relationship between the Greek soul and the Gospel message, there are some resonances that upset us In humanity, amazement should not disappear, for it is the faculty to be surprised and to listen that poses no questions about utility alone, but sees the harmony of the spheres and rejoices at what is of no immediate service to humanity.

Let us go further. To be a child means to say "Father,"

as we have already stated. It is now necessary for us to add that to be a child also means to say "Mother." If we suppress this fact, we are at the same time suppressing the human childhood of Jesus. We are only allowing the sonship of the Word to exist. Yet this sonship should be made accessible to us through the child Jesus. Hans Ur von Balthasar gave a magnificent formulation of this idea which is worthwhile quoting in its entirety:

> *Eucharistia* means thanksgiving. How strange it is that Jesus gives thanks as he constantly offers himself and gives himself to God and to human beings. But whom is he thanking? Quite certainly he is thanking God the Father, the first model and origin of every gift. . . . But he is also thanking the poor sinners who wish to welcome him and allow him to enter under their unworthy roof. Does he thank anyone else? I really think that he thanks the poor serving girl from whom he received his flesh and blood, the girl the Holy Spirit took under his shadow. . . . What does Jesus learn from his mother? He learns how to say yes. Not just any yes, but a yes that always goes further, untiringly. Everything you wish, My God. . . . "Behold the handmaid of the Lord; be it done unto me according to thy word. . . ." This is the Catholic prayer that Jesus learned from his mother according to the flesh, from the *Catholica Mater* who was in the world before him and whom God inspired to pronounce first of all that word of the New and Eternal Covenant.[8]

In the writings of Stylianos Harkianakis we find in this connection a statement that gives to the logic of a child so pure and convincing a form that beside it all rational explanations can only be pale abstractions devoid of the brilliance of a child's glance:

A monk of the cloister at Iviron told me one day: "We

THE GOD OF JESUS CHRIST

venerate the Mother of God and have placed all our hope
in her, for we know that she can do everything. And do you
know why she can? Her Son leaves none of her desires un-
fulfilled because he has never given back to her what he
borrowed. He received from her the flesh that he has certainly glorified — but has never given it back. This is why
we feel ourselves so secure in the garden of the Mother of
God.[9]

2. Nazareth

Nazareth has been hidden from us by the painters of
the "Nazarean School." This term evokes too well the
sentimental way in which the life of Jesus has been changed
into a petit bourgeois idyll that is deceptive because it at-
tenuates the mystery. We have to seek elsewhere the source
of our veneration for the Holy Family, which in turn does
not usually escape the same verdict. During the eighteenth
century, Cardinal Laval of Canada fostered this veneration
by appealing to the responsibility of the laity. The cardinal:

> recognized then the necessity of giving to the colonial popu-
> lation a solid social basis to prevent it from falling into
> danger because of its lack of roots and tradition. He did not
> have enough priests to found formal eucharistic communi-
> ties. . . . Therefore he directed all his attention to the family:
> the life of prayer was entrusted to the father of the fam-
> ily. . . .[10]

Starting with Nazareth we discover that the home and the
family are a church, and that we should take into account
the sacerdotal responsibility of the head of the family. In
"pagan Galilee" Jesus received a Jewish education. Without going to school he came to know Scripture in the

home where the hearth of the Word of God is found.[11] The scanty allusions in Luke's Gospel are enough to give us an idea of the spirit of responsibility and openness as well as of the fervor and honesty typical of that home community; this spirit made it a realization of the true Israel. We recognize above all in the actions of Jesus, who read the Scriptures and knew them with the assurance of a master — just as he dominated the rabbinical tradition — how much the common life of Nazareth was fruitful for his training. And should all of this be of no concern at all to us who are in a period when most Christians are obliged to live in our own "pagan Galilee"? The universal Church can neither believe nor prosper if we fail to make it aware of the fact that its roots lie hidden in the atmosphere of Nazareth.

A new viewpoint on this subject is unavoidable. While sentimentalism about Nazareth was still flourishing, the true mystery of Nazareth's real content was discovered in a new way — and people living at the time knew nothing about it. In his search for the "last place," Charles de Foucauld discovered Nazareth.* During his pilgrimage to the Holy Land, this place most impressed him. He did not feel himself called to "walk after Jesus in his public life. Nazareth was what gripped him in the depths of his heart."[12] He wanted to follow the silent, poor, hard-working Jesus. He wanted to accomplish to the letter Jesus' advice: "But when thou are invited, go and recline in the last place" (Luke 14:10). He knew that Jesus himself

---

*Charles de Foucauld (1858–1916), French army officer and explorer. Ordained a priest in 1901, he became a hermit in the Sahara, and was killed by Muslim tribesmen. — *Trans.*

had given the explanation of this statement by first doing it. He knew that before Jesus died on the cross, naked and destitute, he had chosen Nazareth as the last place.

Charles de Foucauld first found his Nazareth in the Trappist community of Our Lady of the Snows [*Notre-Dame-des-Neiges*] in 1890. Then only six months later he found it in Syria in an even poorer Trappist community, Our Lady of the Sacred Heart [*Notre-Dame-du-Sacré Coeur*]. From this place he wrote his sister:

> We are doing the work of peasants — work infinitely salutary for the soul, during which we can pray and meditate. . . . We understand so well what a morsel of bread is because we know by experience how much effort is needed to make it. . . .[13]

By retracing the footsteps of the "mysteries of Jesus' life." Charles de Foucauld found Jesus the worker. He met the real "historical Jesus." In 1892, while Charles de Foucauld was working at our Lady of the Sacred Heart, a book by Martin Kähler was published in Europe, *The So-called Historical Jesus and the Historical, Biblical Christ* [*Der sogenannte historische Jesus und der geschichtliche, biblische Christus*]. It was a sensation — one of the first peaks in the debate over the Jesus of history. Brother Charles knew nothing about all this in his Trappist community in Syria. But by entering into the experience of Nazareth, he learned more about it than all the learned discussion could illuminate. Out there, in his living meditation over Jesus, a new path was thus opened up even for the Church. For to work with Jesus the worker and to immerse himself in "Nazareth" was a departure point to both the concept and the reality of the worker-priests. For the Church it was a rediscovery of poverty. Nazareth had a permanent message for the Church. The New Covenant did not begin in the temple nor on the holy mountain; it began in the little dwelling of the Virgin, the house of the worker, and one of the forgotten places of "pagan Galilee" from which no good could be expected. Only from this point could the Church take its new departure and heal itself. The Church will never be able to furnish the right response to our century's rebellion against the power of wealth unless in its own bosom Nazareth becomes a reality that is lived.

3. Public Life and Intimacy

Christ's period of silence, apprenticeship, and waiting was followed by action and his entrance into public life. Being a man meant for Jesus taking part in the joy and success that public life could give him and in the happiness of a human undertaking that might lead to success. But it meant also taking part in the responsibilities and dangers linked to public life. Whoever acts in public does not only make friends but also exposes himself to contradiction, incomprehension, and abuse. His name and his word can then be used by parties on the right as well as on the left. The Antichrist makes use of the mask of Christ and will employ this procedure just as the Devil makes use of the Word of God, which is the Bible (Matt. 4: 1–4; Luke 4: 1–13). Public life is also paradoxically a kind of isolation. And so it was for Jesus. He gathered some friends, but the disappointment of a friendship that was betrayed was not spared him, nor the disappointment of being misunderstood by his Apostles who were men of good will but weak. In the end he was to live alone on the Mount of Olives the hour of agony during which his disciples were asleep. He was misunderstood in his innermost nature.

In addition to the solitude due to a lack of understanding, there was for Jesus another way of being alone. He lived his life by beginning from a center that others could not reach: his solitude with God. In him was verified more than in anyone else a statement of Guillaume de Saint-Thierry: "Whoever is with God is never less alone than when he is alone."[14] Among the evangelists Luke handled this topic with the greatest insight. For this reason I would like to analyze briefly three significant passages in Luke's Gospel. First, however, let us examine a passage in Mark's Gospel that demonstrates how Luke, even if he has special accents all his own, still remained in the common tradition of all the evangelists.

Let us begin then with Mark 6: 45–52 (cf. Matt. 14: 22–23). Mark relates how, after the miracle of the multiplication of the loaves of bread, Jesus withdrew all alone on "the" mountain to pray. The Apostles crossed the lake. He alone was on land, while they were out rowing without making any progress because the wind was against them. Jesus prayed and in his prayer he *saw* them strive to make headway. Then he came to meet them. It is clear that this passage is full of ecclesiological symbols: The Apostles are shown at sea and struggling against the wind, and the Lord is shown as absorbed in the Father. But the decisive aspect is that, when Jesus was with the Father in prayer, he was not absent. On the contrary, in praying he saw his Apostles. When Jesus is with the Father, he is present in the Church. In this passage the problem of the Parousia was examined thoroughly and transformed in a trinitarian manner. Jesus saw the Church in the Father and, by the power of the Father and the strength of his dialogue with him, he himself was present to the Church. It was precisely his dialogue with the Father when he was "on the mountain," that made him present, and the other way around: the Church was, so to speak, the object of the conversation between the Father and the Son, and thus the Church was firmly fixed in the life of the Trinity.

The first text of Luke I would like to present has to do with the calling of the Twelve (Luke 6: 12–16). In Luke's account this call was the result of a night of prayer. In this connection we recall the fine expression of St. Ambrose: "Jesus has spent the whole night praying for you. And what are you doing for your own salvation?" It is especially meaningful to note the difference between Luke's passage and the version of the same event related by Matthew. In Matthew's account the calling of the Twelve followed Jesus' invitation to the disciples to request workers for the harvest. The choice of the Twelve then was like a first sign that this prayer has been granted. In this sign Jesus himself gave, by way of anticipation, the response of divine omnipotence to the Apostles' prayer. In Luke's account, on the other hand, the night prayer of the Lord on the mountain was the inner occasion for the calling of the Apostles. In his solitary dialogue with the Father was found, in the strict sense of the term, the *theo*-logical occasion of the apostolate. If we put the matter the other way around, it is clear that the apostolate had a theological occasion. It proceeded from the exchange between the will of the Father and the will of the Son, and remained sheltered there.

In the second place I shall invoke Luke's version of the

Transfiguration (Luke 9: 28–36). According to Luke, the Transfiguration of Jesus took place as he was praying. As he prayed, his countenance was transformed. . . . In prayer the heart of the mystery of Jesus appeared. We see clearly who he truly is. Some have seen in this narrative an account of the Resurrection, projected in advance into the lifetime of Jesus. But perhaps it is necessary to make a more precise statement: a "manifestation of the Resurrection." An apparition coming from the Father and accompanied by glory could have taken place before the Resurrection because the inner basis of the Resurrection was already present in Jesus on earth. This was made possible by the immersion of the heart of his existence in his dialogue with the Father, which was both the glory of the Son and the very content of his sonship. His passion and death would mean then that his entire earthly existence was remolded and was consumed in a total dialogue of love.

With this as our departure point, we can say that Luke raised the prayer of Jesus to the rank of an essential christological category. Starting out from this point, he described the mystery of the Son. What the Council of Chalcedon expressed in a formula drawn from Greek ontology, Luke said by using a quite personal category that began with the historical experience of the earthly Jesus. As for the formula itself, there exists a perfect correspondence with the formula of Chalcedon. This point is verified in a third passage: the main profession of faith that Peter made to Christ, which Matthew placed at Caesarea Philippi and which he tied again to the promise of Peter's primacy. This profession of faith in Luke 9:18 was the result of Jesus' prayer and was its reply. It almost allows us to understand what happened in Jesus' prayer:

> And it came to pass as he was praying in private, that
> his disciples also were with him, and he asked them, saying,
> "Who do the crowds say that I am?"

The paradox of this passage is obvious; while he was alone, his disciples were with him. That deliberate contradiction reveals that there is in this account no coherency of a historical order but one of a theological order. Those who did not know his privacy took it for one thing or another. Peter's profession of faith expresses the very being of Jesus: It is a glimpse that penetrates into what is characteristic of Jesus — his solitary dialogue with the Father. The profession of faith can only make progress by taking part in Jesus' solitude when we "are with him," that is, with him who is alone with the Father. The public action of Jesus had its center in this intimacy through which his public work embraces the entire world. From this intimacy Jesus comes to humanity, in it he is with human beings, and in it human beings reach him.

4. Death and Resurrection

To be a human being means to be marked for death. To be a human being means to be obliged to die. Humanity is full of contradictions, and according to our biological situation it is natural and necessary for us to die. For humanity, however, a spiritual center aspiring to eternity has opened in the biological sphere. From this viewpoint dying is not natural but illogical. For dying means being rejected from the domain of love, and it means destroying a communication that was made to last.

Living in this world means dying. "He became man" thus means also that he went toward death. This contradiction, which is peculiar to the death of a human being, reached in Jesus its high point. For in him, who was in total communion with the Father, the absolute isolation of death was a pure absurdity. On the other hand, in him death also was a necessity. In fact, we have already seen that his being with the Father was the very reason for the lack of understanding human beings showed him, and it was the reason for his solitude among crowds. His condemnation was the final result of the failure to understand him; it was the casting off into a zone of silence of a person who could not be understood.

At the same time we can perhaps glimpse something of the inner, theological dimension of his death. For dying in a human being is always both a biological and a humano-spiritual event. In Christ's death the destruction of the bodily props of communication broke the dialogue with the Father. If the bodily prop is destroyed, at the same time the spiritual action dependent on it disappears. What was broken was more important than in any ordinary human death. What was ripped away was the dialogue that is, in fact, the axis of the whole world. The cry of suffering in Psalm 21 — "My God, my God, why have you forsaken me?" — lets us perceive something of the unfathomable character of this process. Just as this dialogue had made Jesus solitary and was the basis for the monstrous quality of his death, in the same way the Resurrection was already basically present in it. For through the Resurrection his condition as a man is inserted into the triune exchange of eternal love. It could never disappear again.

Beyond the threshold of death, it rose again and recreated its fullness.

Only the Resurrection thus unveiled the ultimate and decisive character of that article of faith: "he became man." Setting out from it, we know that this expression has validity forever: he *is* a man and remains one forever. The human condition entered through him into the very being of God, and is the fruit of his death. We are *in* God. God is both the Other and the Non-Other.[15] When we say with him Father, we say it in God himself. And this is humanity's hope, this is Christian joy, this is the good news: He is still a man today. In him God has truly become the Non-Other. Human beings — those absurd creatures — are no longer absurd; we have the right to rejoice for God loves us. He loves us so much that his love became flesh and remains flesh. That joy should be the strongest and greatest impulse inciting us to share all this with other human beings to make them happy too by virtue of the light that rose for us and which, in the middle of the night of the world, announces the day.

ONE IN BEING WITH THE FATHER

In 1975 the commemoration of the first ecumenical council — the Council of Nicaea — was celebrated in many places. Through this council the faith of the Church definitively assured itself of the divinity of Jesus by adding to the Creed a single philosophical word: *homoousios* [one in Being with the Father]. In the debate over Christology with which we again find ourselves confronted today, the commemoration of this council is thus something quite up to date. This appears in some issues that at first glance still seem to indicate that that council is not at all of current interest. For example, how can words that come to us out of such a distant past still have any meaning today? How can these issues still concern us, and how can these responses still help us? Is it useful to celebrate the past? Isn't it more valuable to arm ourselves with a view to the present and the future?

Whoever examines Nicaea more closely will be more than ever convinced in these suspicions. This council defined the divine sonship of Jesus. But isn't that what removes Jesus from us by making him inaccessible to us? Isn't it the man Jesus whom we are still capable of understanding, and who is still of interest to human beings today? Isn't it time to turn away from the pomp of divinity to draw out of our love for the man Jesus a love for the human condition that is appropriate to our own period of history? The principal word of the council was *homoousios* — Jesus is one in Being with the Father. Doesn't this confirm once again our suspicions? Doesn't it mean that a kind of philosophy has been constructed from our faith? At that time this was perhaps inevitable, but how can it concern us now? Wasn't our faith handed over to the Greek inquiry about Being, whereas it would have been more biblical and more modern to be concerned about human history in which we ourselves are involved and which sends out to us an urgent request for help?

For anyone who does not stop at the surface of things, quite different questions will arise without delay. However clear everything I've just said may be, isn't this a kind of flight before the greatness of the One who is coming to meet us? After the Council of Chalcedon, Emperor Leo I conducted an inquiry among the bishops to find out what they thought of the decisions taken at this gathering of the churches. Thirty-four signed responses of some 280 bishops or monks at the council have survived in a document, the *Codex Encyclius.* One of the bishops who gave his opinion summed up the spirit of the whole document when he stated that it was important for them as bishops to reply *"piscatorie et non aristotelice"* — that is, like fishermen and not like philosophers.[16] This expression might just as well have been made by one of the Fathers at the Council of Nicaea, for it characterized the state of mind which, in the presence of the Arian temptation, provided the bishops with a sense of direction. What was important for them was not the increasingly subtle issues of scholars but rather the simple elements that disappeared behind these issues, the quite simple and primordial questions of simple people. Although the philosophical panorama constantly changes, it is in the nature of these questions to stay the same because the basic elements of humanity — the human nucleus in its simplicity — always stays the same. The more closely issues approach that nucleus, the more do they stay in the very center of our human condition; the simpler they are, the less likely are they to become obsolete. *"Piscatorie, non aristotelice"*: Should we then no longer wonder who Jesus really was?

Is it a matter of indifference to us if he was a man, or more than a man? This can only be the case if at the outset we have eliminated the second solution.

But what was Jesus, and what is he, if he really was only a human being like ourselves? Can we predict with such confidence that Jesus will last? Doesn't he rather sustain himself on the pomp of the faith that has given him his importance through the ages? Isn't he doomed to a rapid end as soon as this pomp disappears? If nothing remains except the man Jesus, then the man himself will not remain for long. Karl Jaspers, who had the attitude of a philosopher in the Christian tradition, tried to keep Jesus' importance by making him the measure of man. But what remained was only an exceptional existence that could not directly indicate a way for others. What remained was hollow and basically meaningless. There is no philosophy of Jesus as a man that in the end has not undergone the same fate. If he remained only a man, the man himself did not remain. What gives Jesus his importance and makes him irreplaceable for all time is precisely the fact that he was and is the Son, and that in him God became man. God does not oust the man, but he alone gives him his value and confers on him an infinite importance. To eliminate God does not mean discovering the man Jesus, but on the contrary it means smothering him for the benefit of ideals of short duration that we ourselves have fabricated. Who Jesus was is a question of fishermen, not a problem of ontology that is alien to us. No modification could cause this issue to become obsolete or in vain. If Jesus was God, if in him God became man, then something really happened in him. Only then was the skeptical and melancholy phrase of Ecclesiastes — "There is nothing

new under the sun" — made obsolete. Only then did
something take place, for no history at all could have
occurred unless it were true that Jesus *is* the Son of God.
It is precisely this fact of his being that constitutes the
unbelievable event from which everything else depends.

But why was Arius' reply so terribly evident to the
people of his time? Why did he sway so rapidly the minds
of the entire cultivated world? For the same reasons that
the Council of Nicaea is still rejected by public opinion.
Arius wanted to preserve the purity of the concept of
God. He did not want to attribute to God anything so
naive as the Incarnation. He was convinced that in the
end it was absolutely unnecessary to mix up the notion of
God, God himself, and human history. He was of the
opinion that in the last instance the world had to regulate
its affairs by itself, and that it could in no way approach
God, and that God himself was too great to be able to
enter into contact with the world. The Fathers regarded
this view as atheism, and in the end this is correct because
a God whom humanity cannot in any way approach and
a God who cannot play a real role in the world is not a
God. But haven't we long ago gone back quite quietly to
an atheism of the same type? Doesn't it seem to us in-
tolerable to lower God to the human condition, and doesn't
it seem to us impossible that human beings can truly accomplish something with God in the world? Isn't this the
reason that we have passionately turned to the man Jesus?
But we have ended up with a philosophy of despair, for if
God has no power in the world, and if we alone have
power, what remains except despair — a despair that hides
itself under a lot of big words?

"*Piscatorie, non aristotelice*" — this is fine, we say. The

Fathers of Nicaea, in fact, asked some questions as fishermen and not as philosophers. Therefore, they also asked our own questions — the most profound questions that cannot become obsolete. But did they really respond like fishermen and not like Aristotelians? Is *homoousios* the response of fishermen? Doesn't it rather smack of Aristotle and thus of the past? Everything seems to agree with such an interpretation. But what are we really concerned about? Among the numerous titles with which our faith has right away from the start encompassed the mystery of Jesus, a single and unique title emerged increasingly during the elaboration of the profession of faith as the nucleus that contained everything else. It was the word *Son*. Rooted in Jesus' prayer, this word refers to the deep intimacy of himself. But as seen through human thought, it remains an image applied to God. What is its meaning? To what extent have we the right to take it literally, and should we do so? The whole world is no longer the same, and my life and the lives of all of us change completely according to whether we are concerned with religious lyricism or an extremely serious affirmation. The little word *homoousios* was in the eyes of the Fathers of Nicaea only the transposition of the image of the Son into a concept. This word, which means simply Son, is not only a comparison but also a literal reality. The very heart of the Bible — its witness about Jesus Christ — is to be taken literally. The word is to be taken by the letter — it means simply to call Jesus one in Being with the Father. It is not a question of adding some philosophy to the Bible, but it is rather a protection against the ascendancy of philosophy. This serves to protect its literal meaning in the hermeneutical dispute. What the Fathers really said in it was a reply of fishermen: The word is to be taken at its own word. It is valid for what it is. The boldness and greatness of this expression are quite different from a human effort to seek a concept. Abandoning the dispute about concepts, it brings us back to the very heart of the word. Its simplicity is its worth and because of this it achieves a greatness that stirs us. It is not an idea but a reality. The Son is truly the Son. This is why the martyrs died, this is what Christians of all periods have lived from. Only this reality endures.[17]

Whence does the Church receive the courage to make such a profession of faith? And who can point out its way to us? As a conclusion to these reflections, let us hasten to the response the Lord himself made:

> I praise thee, Father, Lord of heaven and earth, that thou didst hide these things from the wise and prudent, and didst reveal them to little ones. Yes, Father, for such was thy good pleasure. All things have been delivered to me by my Father; and no one knows the Son except that Father; nor does anyone know the Father except the Son, and him to whom the Son chooses to reveal him" (Matt. 11: 25–27).

What does this mean? Right off something quite simple and clear has been said. God is recognized only by God. No one can know God beside God himself. The knowledge by which God knows himself is a gift God makes of himself as the Father. It is a movement by which God receives himself and gives himself as the Son. It is an exchange of eternal love, that is, both an eternal gift and a gift in return. Because this is the case, the one "to whom the Son chooses to reveal him" can also recognize him. The will of the Son is not arbitrary like the will of tyrants or the great of this world. The person who is in accord with the will of the Son is one who through God's mercy lives in the state of mind of the Son — this person has not divested himself or herself of the mystery of childhood and has not become so emancipated or established that he or she cannot say "Father," and cannot offer thanks or give himself or herself in return. This is why there is a secret correspondence between the dependency of little ones and knowledge. It is not because Christianity is supposed to be a religion of resentment or a religion of fools, but because the knowledge of God can only blossom if our will is in conformity with the Son's will. A person who wants to be an adult makes himself or herself God, and at the same stroke loses both God and self. But if we continue to say "Father," our sonship will come into blossom and with the sonship also our knowledge and freedom — that is, our belonging to God who is our salvation.

"Piscatorie, non aristotelice" — the Fathers of Nicaea did not fear to belong to the crowd of little ones. That is why they could enter into the praises of the Father through which the will of the Son is manifest and becomes a liberation for outcasts. Let us pray to the Son to grant that we too may remain in the kingdom of his will, that we may become sons through the Son who is one in Being with the Father, and that we may receive in this way the freedom of salvation.

HE ROSE AGAIN IN FULFILLMENT OF THE SCRIPTURES [18]

The debate about the Resurrection of Jesus Christ from the dead has been rekindled with renewed strength and is penetrating right into the very heart of the Church. It is fed not only by a general crisis in our traditional values but also quite especially by the form in which these traditions have been transmitted to us. The fact that the biblical texts have had to be translated again — not only at the level of language but also at the level of ideas — from the world of the past to the present world clearly shows that with respect to the Resurrection too we might need a method of translation that would jostle quite a few of our customary ways of representing it. This impression is confirmed if we compare the different accounts of the Resurrection. Their differences then jump out at us, and we see that, although in a stammering fashion, they are trying to translate into words an event for which customary langu-

age quite obviously does not offer adequate ways of expression. We cannot put aside the problem of deciding
what is the heart of the matter and what is just the outer
framework, just as we find it hard to distinguish between
a false translation and a correct one.

In this reflection I do not wish to discuss the different
theories existing today about the Resurrection, but I would
like to do as much as I can so that the recognized nucleus
of the biblical witness can emerge in a positive way.
Whoever reads the New Testament can affirm without
much difficulty that there are two essentially different
accounts of the Resurrection. There is what I should like
to call the *confessing tradition* and what might be desig-
nated as the *narrative tradition*. The first type is represented by verses 3 to 8 of Chapter 15 of the First Epistle
to the Corinthians. We find the second type in the Resurrection accounts of the four Gospels. These two types did
not arise in the same way; they have as their bases quite
different issues; and they have to fulfill quite different
tasks. As a result their aims are also different, and this
is of great importance in interpreting their message and in
knowing what its essential point is.

We can guess at the source of the confessing tradition by
starting out with the narrative tradition. The narrative tradition relates that on their return to Jerusalem the pilgrims
of Emmaus were received by the Eleven, who greeted them
with these words: "The Lord has truly risen, he appeared
to Peter." It is possible that this is the oldest text we have
about the Resurrection.[19] In any case, a tradition began to
be formulated through such simple exclamations, which
little by little in the assembly of the Apostles became a
solid, firmly formulated element. For a time those ex-

clamations were a profession of faith in the Lord, an expression of hope, and at the same time a sign of recognition for believers. The Christian profession of faith was in the process of being formed. Very early in the process of transmission — probably during the 30's in Palestine — the profession of faith was born that Paul preserved for us in 1 Corinthians 15:3-8 as a tradition he had received at first hand which he transmitted in the same way. In the oldest texts it is only very secondarily a matter of what we would call today concepts of faith. As Paul strongly emphasized, the real intention was to maintain the essential Christian nucleus without which both message and faith would be in vain.

The narrative tradition arose as a result of another impulse. People wanted to know how all of this took place. The need for nearness and for details appeared. Very quickly was added the need for Christians to defend themselves against suspicions and against all sorts of attacks we can guess at from reading the Gospel. There was also the need to defend themselves against perversions of the Gospel such as the one that began to flourish at Corinth. This required accounts of a more detailed content. Starting out from such needs, the more extended tradition of the Gospels took form. As a result, each of the two traditions is irreplaceable, but at the same time it is clear that there is a hierarchy and that the confessing tradition is above the narrative tradition. It is the true faith, the standard for every interpretation.

Let us try therefore to understand a little better the basic creed Paul preserved. Every attempt to arrive at solutions in this dispute about opinions should begin at this point. Paul, or rather his creed, begins with the death of Jesus. It is self-evident that this succinct text, which does not say a word too much, includes two additions to the news that "he is dead." The first is "according to the Scriptures," and the second is "for our sins." What does this mean?

The affirmation *according to the Scriptures* inserts the event into the context of the history of the Old Testament covenant of God with his people. This death is not an isolated bit of chance, but it enters into the context of divine history, and receives from it its logic and meaning. It is an event by which the words of Scripture are accomplished, that is to say, an event that includes a Logos or a logic. The Logos comes from the Word, enters into the Word, retrieves it, and accomplishes it. This death results from the coming of the Word of God among human beings.

What we must understand more exactly by this verbal expression is suggested by a second addition. The death was "for our sins." Our Creed takes up again through this formula the words of a prophet (Isa. 53: 12; cf. Isa. 53: 7–11). This harkening back to Scripture had a definite goal; it had an Old Testament resonance that believers were well acquainted with, thanks to testimonial selections of an early date.[20] Objectively, the death of Jesus was thus removed from the lineage of the cursed death that proceeded from the tree of knowledge, that is, from the desire of humanity to become the equal of God. This desire ended in such a way that humanity was nothing but earth and no longer God. Jesus' death was of quite a different order. It was not the accomplishment of a judgment that thrust humanity toward the earth but rather the accomplishment of a love that did not wish to leave others without a

Word, without meaning, without eternity. It was not inscribed in a sentence of judgment at the gate of Paradise
but in the songs of the servant of God; it was a death that
was born of this Word, and thus a death that became a
light for the people. It was a death in association with the
liturgy of expiation that might bring about a reconciliation,
and thus a death that denoted the end of death.

Seen in this light, the double commentary that our
Creed adds to the brief phrase — "he died" — already
points the Cross toward the Resurrection. What it says is
not just a commentary but constitutes an integral part of
the event itself.

Then comes in the text of the Scripture a hard, short
phrase without commentary — "and was buried." We
cannot understand it except by tying it to what precedes
and what follows it. At the outset it means that Jesus endured the fate of death right up to the very end, that he
was placed in the pit of death, and that he went down
into the world of death, that is, to hell. The faith of the
Church has later reflected intensely on this mystery of
the death of Jesus and tried to understand from this starting point the fullness of Jesus' victory that embraced
both history and the world.[21] Today another issue becomes
inescapable: Does the tomb play a role in our faith? Has
it something to do with the Resurrection of the Lord?
Just on this point a sharp difference of opinion is raging —
a dispute over the kind of realism the Christian message
in fact requires. On this matter very relevant reflections
have been made. What is the use of the miracle of the dead
body that has been brought back to life? To whom is it
helpful? Is this conflict with the laws of nature in accord
with the dignity of the divine Word? Doesn't it cause us

to go completely beyond the things that might affect us here and now? With equal quickness some other important yet contrasting questions are raised. The event of the Resurrection has been transformed into our consciousness of a mission to be pursued and of Jesus' permanent meaning. But doesn't this constitute a series of subterfuges that deprive our faith in the Resurrection of its characteristic of reality? In the scornful rejection of what is called the miracle of the dead body that has been brought back to life, isn't there really a scorn for the body that is as un-Christian as it is humanly false? Isn't there hidden in this scorn a certain skepticism that deprives God of every possibility for action in the world? What then is this promise since the body is quite obviously destined for nothingness?

Now we must recognize right away that our Creed does not speak of the empty tomb. The important point is not that the tomb was empty but that Jesus should have rested within it. We must also recognize that, if we seek to understand the Resurrection by deducing it, so to speak, from the tomb, which is to consider it contrary to entombment, this is to miss the meaning of the New Testament message. For Jesus was not just a dead man who has come back to life like the young man of Naim and Lazarus, who were recalled to a life on earth that would later be ended by a definitive death. The Resurrection of Jesus had no connection with a new kind of victory over clinical death, which we also have seen in our own time but which is a victory to be ended eventually by a clinical death from which there can be no recovery.

This was not the case for Jesus, as the evangelists and also our Creed state quite clearly in mentioning the appearance of the resurrected Christ with the Greek word *ôphtè*. This is generally translated as "he appeared," but perhaps we should say more exactly "he let himself be seen." This formula shows that there was something different about the event. After the Resurrection Jesus belongs to a realm of reality that normally escapes our eyes. Only in this way can we explain the inability to recognize Jesus of which all the evangelists speak. He no longer belongs to the world that can be grasped by the senses but to the world of God. Thus he can only be seen by someone by whom he allows himself to be seen. To see him in this way, the heart and mind of human beings as well as an inner openness are drawn upon. Even in everyday life our sight is not such a banal process as we usually suppose. Two individuals looking at the world at the same time rarely see the same thing. We thus always see from within ourselves. According to circumstances, an individual may perceive the beauty of things or only their usefulness. We may read on the countenance of another person concern, love, a hidden distress, or a dissimulation — or we may not perceive anything at all. All this appears in a way equally perceptible to the senses and yet is only perceived in a process both sensory and spiritual. This process demands all the more on our part as the manifestation of something to our senses reaches the basis of reality. The same is true for the risen Lord: He shows himself to the senses, and yet he can only address himself to senses that look beyond what can be perceived by the senses.

With the whole of the text as our starting point, we must say therefore that Jesus certainly was not alive like a dead man who had been brought back to life, but that he held his life from the very nucleus of divine strength, above the realm of what can be measured by physics and chemistry.

At the same time, however, it is also certain that he was truly alive — the individual called Jesus who had been executed two days earlier. Our text states this precisely by citing two phrases, one after the other. It is first said that "he rose again the third day, according to the Scriptures." Then it goes on to affirm that "he appeared to Cephas, then to the Eleven."

The Resurrection and the appearances are distinctly separate and autonomous elements of the profession of faith. The Resurrection does not dissolve into the apparitions. The apparitions are *not* the Resurrection but only its reflection. The Resurrection is in the first place an *event* produced in Jesus himself, between the Father and him through the power of the Holy Spirit. Finally this event that happened to Jesus becomes *accessible* to human beings because he makes it so. And at this point we are brought back to the tomb and now glimpse a response. The tomb is not the center of the message of the Resurrection, but rather this center is the Lord in his new life. All the same, the tomb cannot be disassociated from the message.

If, in this extremely concentrated text, the placement in the tomb is mentioned on purpose and in a lapidary manner, this is to bring out the fact that the burial was not the last stage of Jesus' earthly journey. The formulation that follows, the Resurrection "on the third day, according to the Scriptures," is already a discreet allusion to Psalm 15:10. This psalm is accounted one of the principal elements in the scriptural argument; according to the preachings of the first Christians that the Acts of the Apostles have passed on to us, it is necessary to consider the psalm as the essential point for the phrase "according to the Scriptures." It states: "You will not abandon my soul to the nether world, nor will you suffer your faithful one to undergo corruption."

According to the Jewish viewpoint, decomposition took place after the third day. The word of the Scriptures was accomplished in Jesus inasmuch as he rose again on the third day before decomposition set in. The text is also linked here at the same time to the article in the Creed about death. All this is related to the Scriptures — the new death of Jesus led to the tomb but not to corruption. It was the death of death — death which was included for the Word of God as well as the course of life — it snatches from death its power at the moment when in the earth it dissolves the human being in the destruction of the body.[22]

This victory over the power of death at the very moment when it seemed fully irrevocable was an important point in the biblical testimony. Let us set aside the fact that it would have been completely impossible to announce the Resurrection of Jesus if everyone could have known and affirmed that he was in the tomb. It would be impossible in our society, which works in a theoretical manner on concepts having to do with the Resurrection and for which the body is a matter of indifference. It was even more so in the Jewish world for which a human being was his or her body and nothing else. Whoever recognizes this is not affirming that an astonishing miracle took place, he is affirming the power of God who respects his creature but is not linked to the law of that creature's death. Certainly, death is the basic law of the world as it is at the present time. But the victory over death — its real suppression, not just its suppression in thought — remains today as always an aspiration and quest of humanity. The Resurrection of Jesus tells us that that victory is really possible, that death did not form a part in its very principle and in an irreversable manner of the structure of what is created, that is, of matter. It tells us further that victory on the frontiers of death is impossible of attainment by clinical methods now perfected or by technology. Such a victory exists only through the creative power of the Word and love. Only these powers are sufficiently strong to change the structure of matter so radically that the barriers of death may become surmountable. To this extent the extraordinary promise of the event of the Resurrection contains also an extraordinary appeal and a mission. It is a complete interpretation of the human condition and of the world.

Above all, it is clear, however, that faith in the Resurrection of Jesus is a profession of faith in the real existence of God. It is also a profession of faith in his creation, an unconditional yes that characterizes the relationship of God to creation and matter. The Word of God penetrates truly right into the body. His power does not stop at the frontiers of matter. It *embraces* everything. And this is why when we respond about that Word, we penetrate right into matter and into the body — and we stay there. In faith in the Resurrection, what is at stake in the end is the true power of God and the extent of human responsibility. For the liberating content of the paschal revelation is that the power of God is hope and joy. This is what authorizes us to sing Allelulia in the midst of a world over which the threatening shadow of death hovers.

CHAPTER 3

The Holy Spirit

We believe in God the Father, the Son, and the Holy Spirit, one God in three persons. While we have much to say about the Father and the Son, the Holy Spirit remains the unknown God. Of course, there has always been the appeal to the Holy Spirit in the history of the Church, but the movements born in this way have in the end contributed in different ways to the fact that we speak in the Church more and more discreetly about the Holy Spirit.

Everything began with Mani (216–274 or 277 A.D.), the father of Manichaeism, who arranged to be mistaken for an incarnation of the Paraclete — the Holy Spirit — and thus established his superiority over Christ.[1] From this time on, a shadow fell over the entire history of the Church in the Middle Ages. It was a superior and presumptious form of holiness whose ambitions, although often rejected, darkened the faith of Christendom and became a heritage of which it is difficult to rid ourselves. A spiritual movement that arose from different sources spread through the Church of Asia Minor from the second century on. It was known as Montanism, and its most eloquent representative in the West was the great writer Tertullian (ca. 160–220). Starting out with the message of the Montanists, he felt such scorn for the sinful Church that he ended up in arrogance and moral rigorism.

The most fascinating type of nostalgia for the Holy Spirit was developed by a pious abbott in southern Italy, Joachim of Fiore (ca. 1130–1202).* Joachim felt deeply the insufficiencies of the Church of his time: the hate that divided Jews and Christians, the old and the new people of God; the rivalry between the eastern Church and the western Church; the jealousy between members of the clergy and laity; and the tyranny and lust for power on the part of churchmen. From all this came the conviction that the Church could not be the definitive form of the Church of God on earth. Joachim believed that, before the return of Christ and the end of the world, a new intervention of God would have to take place on earth and in history. He desired a Church that would be truly in conformity with the New Testament, the promises of the prophets, and the most profound aspirations of humanity: a church in which Jews and pagans, East and West, clergy and laity, all would live in the spirit of truth and love without regulations and laws, so that the will of God would be really achieved in his creatures. And so Joachim's new vision of things grew as he tried to interpret the rhythm of history by starting out from the trinitarian image of God. After the age of the Father in the Old Testament and the age of the Son in the Church which up to that time had been hierarchical, there would begin around 1260 A.D. a third age — the age of the Holy Spirit — which would be a realm of liberty and universal peace.

For Joachim such reflections were more than just simple speculations about the future through which he found

---

*Cistercian abbot and mystic of Fiore in Calabria. — *Trans.*

consolation for the miseries of the present age. In his eyes they took on a very practical character, for he believed he had discovered that the different ages did not follow each other by remaining carefully separate from each other. He saw some overlapping in which the thrust of the new age would be already present in the old age. For example, through the faith and piety of the prophets the New Covenant began right in the midst of the Old Covenant. Through the style of life of the monks, the Church of the future was already outlined in the Church of Joachim's day. This had two implications: First of all, we can go to meet what is coming right now, and we can place ourselves in the movement of history as if we were on a moving carpet leading to the future. Joachim himself tried to act in this way by founding a new monastic community that was to be also an anticipation of the new age — a door open onto this new age. Second, Joachim's manner of visualizing the future became clearly outlined. The "everlasting gospel" of which he spoke, referring to the Apocalypse (14: 6), was in the end nothing other than the Gospel of Jesus Christ. The action of the Holy Spirit and his Gospel was rather to be total fulfillment at last of the first Gospel, the Sermon on the Mount. The Gospel taken literally was to constitute the totally spiritual Christianity of the future — such was Joachim's viewpoint.

The hope Joachim had expressed through his reliance on the definitive coming of the Holy Spirit at some future date has ever since kept humanity from peace. First came the Franciscans who saw a new Church in their movement. In the struggles to which this demand gave rise among different tendencies within the Order, the hope lost its spiritual brilliance. This hope became harder and more combative, and in Italy groups seeking a political renewal took possession of it. There is no need here to retrace in detail the history of Joachim's concept. It is remarkable, however, that by different byways Hitler and Mussolini found such slogans as "the Third Reich," "the Führer," and "the Duce" in Joachim's heritage. With Hegel as an intermediary, Marxism also took up some of these views, including the concept of a historical movement that advances in triumph and, in and of itself, attains its goals unerringly. Also involved is the idea of some kind of salvation that establishes itself definitively inside history.[2]

It has been worthwhile to speak in some detail about Joachim because his example serves to bring out the possibilities and dangers of speaking about the Holy Spirit in a certain way. In Joachim's teachings we find some concepts that can guide us, for example, the willingness to begin to live, here and now, a truly "spiritual" form of Christianity as well as the willingness to seek this form of Christianity not in something beyond words but in the deepest meaning of what is spiritual. To a certain extent the first Franciscans were not wholly wrong in viewing Joachim's teaching as a prophetic presentment of the figure of St. Francis. In fact, Francis gave to Joachim the fairest and the only truly correct response. By his life Francis separated the good spirit from the bad spirit of such an action — something his successors were incapable of doing. His maxim was *"sine glossa,"* by which Francis meant that he would live by the Holy Scripture, especially the Sermon on the Mount, and be caught up by the Word literally, without any distinctions or subterfuges. Aspects of Joachim's ideas that were distorted by all sorts of speculations became quite clear in the ideas of Francis of Assisi and

gave rise to the radiant influence Francis has exerted
through the centuries. Christianity in the Spirit is the
Christianity of the Word that we live by. The Spirit dwells
in the Word, and is not in flight from the Word. The
Word is the *locus* of the Spirit: Jesus is the source of the
Spirit. The more we are with Jesus, the more truly are we
with the Spirit who is increasingly with us. And this is
what reveals Joachim's mistake: his utopia about a Church
that departs from the Son in order to raise itself to a higher
level as well as his irrational hope that attempts to pass
itself off as a real and rational program.

Have we not already produced the first sketch of a
theology of the Holy Spirit? The Spirit does not allow
itself to be seen when we depart from the Son. On the
contrary he allows himself to be seen when we are with
the Son, so to speak. John expressed this in a vivid image
in his account of the first appearance of the resurrected
Savior to the Eleven: The Spirit was the breath of the
Son. We receive the Spirit by drawing near to the Son —
within reach of his breath — and then allowing ourselves
to be breathed upon by Jesus (John 20: 19–23). Starting
from this point, St. Irenaeus sketched in a more exact
manner than Joachim the trinitarian logic of history. For
Irenaeus this logic was not an ascension from the Father
to the Son and then to liberation and the Spirit. The direction for individuals takes place within history in exactly
the opposite way. The Spirit is found at the beginning as
the guide and leader of humanity, although he can scarcely
be perceived. He leads us to the Son, and through the Son
he leads us to the Father. . . .

Such knowledge echoes what the Fathers have tried to
say about the nature of the Holy Spirit. The name of the

Third divine Person is certainly not — in contradistinction to the words *Father* and *Son* — an expression of some specific feature. On the contrary, it means what is common to God. Now this is just where what is "proper" to the Third Person appears. This person is what is in common; he is the unity of the Father and the Son; he is the personification of the unity of God. The Father and the Son are *one* to the extent that they go beyond themselves; and they are one in the Third Person, in the fruitfulness of their gift.

Of course, such affirmations can never be anything but mere proximities. We can only recognize the Spirit through his results. Therefore, Scripture never describes the Holy Spirit in himself, but speaks only of the way in which he comes toward humanity and of the way in which he is different from other spirits.

Let us take a look at some of these references in Scripture. In the early Gospel of Pentecost (John 14: 22–31), Judas Thaddeus asked the Lord a question that all of us have brought up in one way or another. From the words of the Lord he surmised that after Christ had risen, he did not wish to show himself to anyone except the disciples. Thus he asked: "Lord, how is it that thou art about to manifest thyself to us, and not to the world?" Jesus' response seemed to go beside the question: "If anyone loves me, he will keep my word, and my Father will love him, and we will come to him and make our abode with him." In fact, it was an exact reply to the disciple's question and to our own question about the Spirit. It is not possible to display the Spirit of God like a piece of merchandise. Only a person who bears God within himself or herself can see him. Seeing and coming, and seeing and staying — these actions go together and are indissociable. The Holy Spirit stays in the Word of Jesus and we do not receive the Word through speeches but through our constancy and through our lives. The Spirit lives in the Word that has been lived and experienced, and he is the life of the Word.

The early Church explored this idea mainly by tying it to Psalm 67, which was regarded as a hymn to the Ascension of Christ and the sending of the Holy Spirit. In the structure of this Old Testament passage, the Church regarded the ascent of Moses as a symbol of what happened at Pentecost. Moses elevated himself not only externally but also internally. He exposed himself to a solitary meeting with God. After enduring the height, the clouds, and the direct, solitary encounter with God, he was able to bring back to human beings the Spirit under the form of a statement that could guide them. The Spirit was the fruit of Moses' ascent and his solitude. From the viewpoint of the New Testament, Moses' way as well as the gift of the Spirit which he brought through the statement of the Law were only a shadowy sketch of what took place in Jesus. Jesus truly introduced human nature — our flesh — into his face-to-face meeting with God. Through the clouds of death he lifted our flesh up to the countenance of God. In this ascent the Spirit came as the fruit of Jesus' victory and as the fruit of his love and the cross.

Starting at this point, we can again try to have a presentation of God's inner mystery. The Father and the Son are a single movement of the pure gift of one to the other; they are a pure offering. In this movement they are fruitful, and their fruitfulness is their unity and their total communion even though their personalities are still not taken from them and they are not dissolved into one another. For us human beings, the offering and the gift of self always mean the cross as well. The mystery of the Trinity is translated in the world into the mystery of the cross; and in it is found the fruitfulness from which the Holy Spirit proceeds.

John forcibly emphasized the fact that the Spirit resides not beside the Word but within it when he named memory as the proper activity of the Spirit in history. The Holy Spirit does not speak of himself but "of what is mine" in Jesus (John 16: 14). He is recognized by his faithfulness to the Word that has been spoken. John constructed in a rigorously parallel fashion his Christology and his teaching about the Spirit. For Christ also is characterized by the fact that he can say: "My teaching is not my own" (John 7: 16). This forgetfulness of self, which is characteristic of him, and the fact that he does not give witness concerning himself — this is what gives Jesus authority with the world. By way of contrast, the Antichrist is recognized by the fact that he speaks in his own name. It is the same also for the Holy Spirit: if he reveals himself to be the Spirit of the Trinity, the Spirit of the one God in three persons, this is precisely because he does not appear as a separate and separable self, but disappears into the Father and the Son. The impossibility of developing a a separate pneumatology (a science of the Spirit) is an integral part of his nature.

John formulated quite knowingly these affirmations within the struggles of his own time as a sign that distinguished the Spirit from the anti-Spirit. The great teachers of gnosis were interesting because of what they said in their own name, and they created a reputation for themselves. They caused a sensation because they had something new and different to say that went beyond the Word. For example, they claimed that Jesus in fact was not dead at all, but that he was dancing with his disciples while people believed him to be hanging on the cross. The fourth Gospel opposed such gnostic novelties and some of their statements that were binding only on those who made them by using the ecclesiastical plural — this disappearance of the one who speaks behind the ecclesiastical "we" really gives to the person who is speaking his true countenance and keeps it from dissolving into nothingness. In John's epistles the same model was followed: the author simply called himself "the presbyter" [elder]. His adversary was the *proagon,* the one who advances (2 John 9). The whole gospel of John as well as his epistles sought to be only a mobilization of memory, and in this respect it is the Gospel of the Holy Spirit. To the extent that his Gospel does not invent something new but recalls its subject by meditating on it, it is fruitful, new, and deep. The nature of the Holy Spirit, which is the unity of the Father and the Son, is forgetfulness of self (in which memory consists). It is the true renewal. A Church of the Spirit is a Church that, by remembering, penetrates more deeply into the Word, and thus becomes more alive and richer. True forgetfulness of self and a detachment from self in order to reach Everything — this is a sign of the Spirit and a copy of his trinitarian nature.

Let us now make a quick survey of Paul's writings on this topic. In the community at Corinth, Paul was confronted by an almost childlike joy in the gifts of the Spirit, but it was a joy that began to threaten what was essential. Everyone wanted to surpass the other. Attention was directed more and more toward what was exterior and the very nature of exterior things. And so the community's attention was slowly moving toward sectarianism. Paul opposed this trend with his insight that only one gift counted — *love* (1 Cor. 13). Without it all the rest was nothing. But love was translated into unity and was the opposite of sectarianism. It revealed itself by building and supporting. Whatever was constructive was the Holy Spirit. Whenever things broke down and wherever bitterness, jealousy, and contention increased, the Holy Spirit was not present. Knowledge without love did not come from him. There was at this point a meeting between Paul's concept and the concept of John, for on the basis of St. John we can say that love appears in constancy. The Pauline teaching about the Body of Christ, in the final analysis, does not say anything else.[3]

On another point Paul and John were also objectively in agreement. John called the Spirit the "Paraclete," which means the advocate, helper, defender, and consoler. The Paraclete was thus opposed to the devil, the "accuser," the calumniator — "he who accused them before our God day and night" (Apoc. 12:10). The Spirit is the yes, just as Christ is the yes. What corresponded to him in Paul's thought was the intensity of the emphasis he placed on joy. The Spirit — we can say it here — is the spirit of joy and the spirit of the Gospel. One of the principal rules for discerning minds might be that wherever there is sadness and wherever humor is dying, the Holy Spirit — the Spirit of Jesus Christ — certainly is not present. And on the contrary, joy is a sign of grace. Whoever is serene in the depths of his or her heart and whoever has suffered without losing joy is not far from the God of the Gospel and from the Spirit of God, which is the Spirit of eternal joy.

Notes

CHAPTER 1

1. Cf. W. Kern, "Tod Gottes und technisches Zeitalter. Umfeld und Vorgeschichte des humanistischen Atheismus," *Stimmen der Zeit* 190 (1970): 219–229. The author places this story and explains it in detail. It is found in a pseudo-epigraph that can be dated from the beginning of the thirteenth century. It originated in Languedoc, and is attributed to the mishna teacher Juda ben Bathyra. Kern shows how the atheistic outcropping that shows up in it is unique in the history of the Golem of the Middle Ages, a time when in any case the possibility of remaking creation passed almost for a demonstration of God's greatness. Cf. also G. Scholem, *La Kabbale et sa symbolique* (Paris: Payot, 1975), pp. 197ff. and all of chap. 5; H. Thielicke, *Der evangelische Glaube I* (Tübingen, 1968) pp. 328–331.

As for the sudden appearance of the question of atheism right in the middle of a religious tradition, I believe that I have found an interesting example in the little prayer book of Duchess Dorothea of Prussia (1531). Verses 7–8 of Psalm 6 "I am wearied with sighing; every night I flood my bed with weeping; I drench my couch with my tears. My eyes are dimmed with sorrow; they have aged because of all my foes." The passage is altered as follows: *"Ich wolt schir liber du werest nit, dann das ich solt lenger also von dir geplagt sein"* [I should prefer that you should not be at all rather than to be thus tormented by you]. Thus, the suffering imposed by God becomes a reason for wishing God's nonexistence. The passage is found in I. Gunderman, *Untersuchungen zum Gebetbüchlein der Herzogin Dorothea von Preussen* (Cologne and Opladen, 1966), Table II, page 39 v of the prayerbook.)

2. Fuller information on religious history can be found in R. Pettazzoni, *Der allwissende Gott* (Frankfurt, 1957). On this very problem see E. Biser, "Atheismus und Theologie" in J. Ratzinger, ed., *Die Frage nach Gott* (Freiburg im Breisgau, 1972), pp. 89–115.

3. Cf. Th. Maertens, *C'est fête en l'honneur de Yahvé* (DDB, 1961), pp. 128–161.

4. For this interpretation see especially R. P. Merendino, *Der unverfügbare Gott. Biblische Erwägungen zur Gottesfrage* (Düsseldorf, 1969); Th. Schneider, *Plädoyer für eine wirkliche Kirche* (Stuttgart, 1972), pp. 24–31; A. Deissler, *Die Grundbotschaft des Alten Testaments* (Freiburg im Breisgau, 1972); J. Ratzinger, *Foi chrétienne hier et aujourd'hui* (Paris: Mame, 1976), pp. 64–78. My student C. del Zotto gave me the idea of placing the name in opposition to the number.

5. Cf. J. Ratzinger, *Dogma und Verkündigung* (Munich, 1973), pp. 40ff.

6. Quoted in *Liturgia horarum iuxta ritum Romanum II* (Vatican City: Typis Polyglottis Vaticanis, 1972), p. 1282; see O. Marcos, *Cartas y escritos de Nuestro Glorioso Padre San Juan de Diós* (Madrid, 1935). Cf. the brief presentation of this personage by H. Firtel in P. Manns, *Die Heiligen* (Mainz, 1975), pp. 481–484. I have made use of this reference to John of God with its reflection of the Beatitudes in order to give concrete details to the preceding passage of the present book.

7. Quoted from *Die Bekenntnisschriften der evangelischlutherischen Kirche* (Göttingen, 1952), p. 560. It is not necessary to treat here of the problems this passage gives rise to, which P. Hacker clarifies well in *Das Ich im Glauben bei Martin Luther* (Graz, 1966), p. 21ff. *The Ego in Faith* (Chicago, Franciscan Herald Press, 1970).

8. What follows is based largely on what I have written in *Dogma und Verkündigung*, pp. 94–98 and 101–104.

9. I have demonstrated this point more in detail in my article "Baptisés dan lá foi de l'Eglise," *Communio*, vol. 1, no. 5 (May 1976), pp. 9–21.

10. M. Buber, *Werke III: Schriften zum Chassidismus* (Munich and Heidelberg, 1963), p. 323.

11. W. Heisenberg, *Der Teil und das Ganze* (Munich, 1969), pp. 118, 293.

NOTES

12. Ibid., p. 293.

13. Ibid., pp. 291, 294.

14. Ibid., p. 295. See also on this point my article "Ich glaube an Gott den Vater, den Allmächtigen, den Schöpfer des Himmels und der Erde," in W. Sandfuchs, ed., *Ich glaube. Vierzehn Betrachtungen, zum Apostolischen Glaubensbekenntnis* (Würzburg, 1975), pp. 13–24.

15. For the best treatment of Marcion, cf. H. Rahner, "Marcion," LThK VII, pp. 92ff.; J. Quasten, *Initiation aux Pères de l'Eglise.* The following are still basic about this personage: A. Harnack, *Marcion: Das Evangelium vom fremden Gott* (Leipzig and Berlin, 1924); *Neue Studien zu Marcion* (Leipzig and Berlin, 1923).

16. Concerning the revolutionary nature of gnosis, cf. H. Jonas, *Gnosis und spätantiker Geist I und II* (Göttingen, 1954); E. Voegelin, *Wissenschaft, Politik und Gnosis* (Munich, 1959).

17. For the implications of the theology of the creation, which are only touched on here, see the fine analysis of P. Schmidt, "La pauvreté du monde," *Revue Catholique Internationale: Communio,* vol. I, no. 3 (January, 1976), pp. 2–14; see also G. Martelet, "Le premier-né de toute créature," ibid., pp. 30–48.

18. This is the way that the disposition of the Holy of Holies is described in Paul's Epistle to the Hebrews 9:4. Concerning the complex problem of the Holy of Holies' real and historical aspect during different stages of the Temple, the basic information is found in A. Van den Born and W. Baier, "Allerheiligstes," in H. Haag, ed., *Bibellexikon* (Einsiedeln, 1968), p. 48.

19. Cf. in this connection what has been said to date in the first meditation.

20. I repeat at this point what I already explained in *Dogma und Verkündigung,* pp. 331–339.

21 This information only mentions but does not give an extensive treatment of the theological profundity of Isaac's sacrifice and his replacement by Christ. To go more deeply into this matter, see L. Massignon, "Les Trois prières d'Abraham," *Parole donnée* (10/18), pp. 277–294.

22. Cf. W. Kornfeld, "Moloch" in H. Haag, ed., *Bibellexikon* (Einsiedeln, 1968), p. 1163ff., and the attached bibliography.

23. *Adv. haer.* IV, 20, 7 (*Sources chrétiennes* 100, p. 648).

CHAPTER 2

1. Concerning the history and contents of the Creed of Nicaea and Constantinople, see J. N. D. Kelly, *Early Christian Creeds* (London, 1950); W. Beinert, *Das Glaubensbekenntnis der Okumene* (Freiburg im Breisgau, 1973); idem, G. Baudler, W. Beinert, A. Kretzer, *Den Glauben bekennen* (Freiburg im Breisgau, 1975), pp. 34–91.

2. Cf. in this connection N. W. Porteous, *Das Buch Daniel* (Göttingen: ATD 23, 1968), pp. 74–96, especially p. 79ff.

3. In the Old Testament the "sphere of death" meant "hell." Cf. H. J. Kraus, *Psalmen I* (Neukirchen, 1960), pp. 305–310, as quoted on p. 307. In the New Testament this passage did not become fully realistic except in association with the real death and real Resurrection of Christ; by replacing this statement before the Incarnation in a dialogue inside the divinity, as is the case here, it takes on new dimensions.

4. There is a good historical overview of this matter in A. Grillmeier, *Mit ihm und in ihm. Christologische Forschungen und Perspektiven* (Freiburg im Breisgau, 1975), pp. 716–736.

5. This is a question that only meditation can encompass since it cannot be explored in a philosophical manner. See the detailed analysis by F. Ulrich, *Der Mensch als Anfang. Zur philosophischen Anthropologie der Kindheit* (Einsiedeln, 1970).

6. J. Jeremias, *Théologie du Nouveau Testament I: La Prédication de Jésus* (Paris: Cerf, 1973), p. 150, which states: "To become a child again means to learn to say again 'Abba-Father.' "

7. St. Harkianakis, *Orthodoxe Kirche und Katholizismus* (Munich, 1975), p. 60ff. The passage in Plato's *Timaeus* — the dialogue between an Egyptian priest and Solon — seems to be shaded differently, it seems to me, in the original text. This, however, is not the place to insist on this point.

8. H. U. von Balthasar, "Haus des Gebetes," in W. Seidel, *Kirche aus lebendigen Steinem* (Mainz, 1975), pp. 11–29, quoted from p. 25ff.

9. Harkianakis, ibid., p. 65.

10. Th. Maertens and J. Frisque, *Guide de l'assemblée chrétienne I* (Casterman, 1965).

11. Cf. on Jesus' early years the impressive developments based on archaeological findings in B. Schwank, "Das Theater von Sepphoris und die Jugendjahre Jesu" in *Erbe und Auftrag 52*

NOTES

(1976), pp. 199–206. The article makes valuable corrections to the customary picture of Judaism in the time of Jesus, and it runs counter to recent Jewish research about Jesus. It is also worthwhile to read Robert Aron, *Les Années obscures de Jésus* (Paris: Grasset, 1960).

12. M. Carrouges, *Charles de Foucauld, explorateur mystique* (Paris: Cerf, 1958), p. 93.

13. Ibid., p. 106.

14. *Lettre d'Or* I, 4, 10.

15. Cf. H. U. von Balthasar, "Evangelium und Philosophie," *Freiburger Zeitschr. f. Philosophie und Theologie* 23 (1976): 3–12.

16. For additional details about the *Codex Encyclius* and its theological content, see A. Grillmeier, *Mit ihm und in ihm,* op. cit., pp. 283–300.

17. Concerning this explanation, see *Internationale Theologenkommission: Die Einheit des Glaubens und der theologische Pluralismus* (Einsiedeln, 1973), pp. 61–67, especially p. 65ff.

18. A recent bibliography of publications about this question in German was drawn up by L. Scheffczyk, *Auferstehung. Prinzip christlichen Glaubens* (Einsiedeln, 1976); on the exegetical discussion see especially B. Rigaux, *Dieu l'a ressuscité* (Duculot, Grembloux, 1973).

19. Cf. H. Schlier, *La résurrection de Jésus Christ* (Paris: Salvator, 1969), especially p. 7; J. Jeremias, *Théologie du Nouveau Testament I: La Prédication de Jésus* (Paris: Cerf, 1973).

20. Concerning the testimonial selections of the early Christians, cf. J. Daniélou, *Etudes d'exégèse judéo-chrétienne* (les Testimonia) (Beauchesne, 1966).

21. Concerning the problem brought up here of Jesus' descent into Hades, see especially H. U. von Balthasar, *Le Mystère pascal, IV: Parmi les morts* (Paris, 1976), pp. 139–177 (Mysterium Salutis 12) and *Pneuma und Institution. Skizzen zur Theologie IV* (Einsiedeln, 1974), pp. 387–400.

22. Cf. J. Kremer, *Das älteste Zeugnis von der Auferstehung Christi* (Stuttgart, 1966), pp. 37–54; concerning the third day see especially K. Lehmann, *Auferweckt am dritten Tag nach der Schrift* (Freiburg im Breisgau, 1968); J. Blank, *Paulus und Jesus* (Munich, 1968), pp. 153–156, and on Pauline faith in the Resurrection, pp. 133–183.

CHAPTER 3

1. Concerning Mani and Manichaeism, see A. Adam, *Lehrbuch der Dogmengeschichte I* (Gütersloh, 1965), pp. 207–210; H.-Ch. Puech, *LThK VI*, pp. 1351–1355.

2. On Joachim of Fiore and his repercussions see especially E. Benz, *Ecclesia spiritualis: Kirchenidee und Geschichtstheologie der franziskanischen Reformation* (Stuttgart, 1934); K. Löwith, *Weltgeschichte und Heilgeschehen* (Stuttgart, 1953), pp. 136–147; A. Dempf, *Sacrum Imperium* (1929, Darmstadt, 1954), especially pp. 269–284. Concerning the acceptance and transformation of Joachim of Fiore's concepts by Franciscan theology, see my *Die Geschichtstheologie des heiligen Bonaventura* (Munich and Zurich, 1959), *The Theology of Bonaventure* (Chicago: Franciscan Herald Press, 1965). For a theological-historical outline of St. Irenaeus, which is opposed to the one given here, see the thesis of R. Tremblay that is to be published in the near future, *La manifestation et la vision de Dieu selon saint Irénée de Lyon*.

3. Concerning these statements, see my article "Die Heilige Geist als communio. Zum Verhältnis von Pneumatologie und Spiritualität bei Augustinus," in C. Heitmann and H. Muhlen, eds., *Erfahrung und Theologie des Heiligen Geistes* (Hamburg and Munich, 1974), pp. 223–238; in addition, concerning the Holy Spirit I refer readers to the entire work and its different interpretations; finally, basic to the science of the Holy Spirit is M. J. Le Guillou, *Les Témoins sont parmi nous. L'expérience de Dieu dans l'Esprit-Saint* (Paris: Fayard, 1976).